SAHARA

Text and Photographs
by Kazuyoshi Nomachi

GROSSET & DUNLAP
A FILMWAYS COMPANY
Publishers · New York

First published in the United States in 1978
by Grosset & Dunlap, Inc., 51 Madison Avenue,
New York 10010.

Library of Congress catalog card number: 77-95324
ISBN 0-448-14729-7

Color separations by A. Mondadori Editore, Verona.
Printed and bound in Italy by A. Mondadori Editore, Verona.

CONTENTS

PREFACE

I first set foot in the Sahara in February, 1972. On that trip a friend and I simply wandered about, with no special aim and no background knowledge. But I soon fell under the spell of the desert and have now visited the Sahara five times, spending a total of thirteen months there.

I have had many different experiences. As for that first trip, I was with six friends in Paris after a skiing tour of Austria and Switzerland when it suddenly occurred to my good friend Izukura and me that it might be a good idea to visit the Sahara before going home. We pooled our meager resources and began making plans. Just when we realized we couldn't even afford to buy a used car for the trip and were about to give up the plan, another of our friends, Sato, who was planning to go to Greece, collapsed from exhaustion due to much skiing. We put him on a plane for Tokyo, and he left with us the money he had saved for Greece.

So we finally got a beat-up old car and set out for Africa. But time had been lost and we had only three weeks left for our trip. We decided to drive night and day. Then, just before dawn on the third day, I evidently dozed at the wheel and must have crossed the center line. By the time I realized this and turned the steering-wheel back, it was already too late. Our Citroën had received a deep gash from the bumper of a large truck going in the opposite direction. The damage certainly didn't make the jalopy look any better, but it would still run, and on we went to Africa. If the gash had been about an inch deeper it would have pierced the gas tank and that would have been the end of our Sahara trip — to say nothing of the possibility that we might have been burned to death and become material for a back-page news item.

Finally, returning from our Sahara jaunt, the car gave out completely. We abandoned it in Spain, at Motril (it had served its purpose valiantly and I've often wondered what finally happened to it), and caught a train to Paris. I was leaving the Sahara, but it remained in my blood.

That accident we had in France was the only real trouble I have encountered during all my trips to or in the Sahara. But not everyone is so lucky. On my fourth trip, in the spring of 1975,

with my wife Shigeko, we left Tamanrasset, bound for Agadez though the scorching desert heat. Two microbuses with German license plates had left Tamanrasset a short time before us. We passed them at noon, while the passengers were eating lunch, and a short time later we looked back to see smoke rising. Going back, we found that one of the buses had caught fire from the gas used in preparing lunch. Two of the men had been burned, not seriously but painfully, and sat groaning in the shadow of the other bus. Meanwhile, the gas tanks of the burning bus, filled with almost three hundred liters of gasoline, started exploding one by one. The bus burned for almost two hours and nothing but a blackened skeleton remained. We made space for two of the Germans — Peter and Wolfram — in our car and the rest managed to squeeze into the remaining microbus. We all drove the three hundred sixty miles to Agadez, where Peter and the other bus-less people, greatly disappointed, took a plane back to Munich.

The nickname of the burned bus was "Panic," they told us. I suppose its blackened form still lies in the desert to remind passing travelers how the Sahara can suddenly betray the highest hopes.

Later that year, after we had finished our tour of the Sahara, we went to Munich where we met Peter again, and he took the Land Rover off our hands. As he told me later, he was still determined to see the Sahara, and set off a while later in our Land Rover. But again there was an accident. They were deep into Niger when an engine valve burned out. They left the car at a garage to be repaired and again returned to Munich by air. Maybe they had even christened the Land Rover "Panic II."

They are still planning to go back to get the car and finish their Sahara travels. I pray their karma be kind. Surely this third time they will return to Munich without incident, having realized their ambition.

It is said that travelers in the Sahara can be divided into two irreconcilable types by their reaction to the desert. One type of person no sooner steps into the desert, smells the odor of death in the barrenness of nature existing in intolerable silence, than he immediately shows symptoms of complete rejection. The other type quickly finds the greatest pleasure and comfort in that vast, arid land. Most of the people who live in the oases belong to the first type, as do the travelers who, though they come to the desert of their own free will, are soon appalled by the harsh conditions and quickly make a U-turn for the Mediterranean and home.

Needless to say, I myself belong to the second type.

Notes on the Photography

The most difficult thing about photography in the desert is taking care of the film in temperatures that can run as high as 122° F (50° C) in the shade. This was the reading of the thermometer we carried in our car. In the closed trunk, where the film was kept, it must have been ten or twenty degrees higher.

At first we thought of storing the film in a refrigerator that would run on the car's battery. But such a refrigerator would have been too small to hold enough film. So instead, we had to content ourselves with trying to keep the film as cool as possible by opening the trunk at each stop when the outside air became a bit cooler. Luckily, because of the extreme dryness of the desert, this measure proved more effective than we had hoped.

I always sent the exposed film off to be developed as quickly as possible, for the most critical period is between exposure and development. Smaller oases seldom have post offices, however, and those that do are not equipped to handle overseas parcels. I often had to wait until we reached larger towns to mail my film. So I usually sent five or ten rolls of exposed film at a time to Kodak in Lausanne, Switzerland, or to Fuji in Tokyo. I mailed such parcels I don't know how many times and — much to the amazement of people who have had experience with Saharan mail service — not once did they fail to reach their destination in good order.

Thus I usually was able to keep color changes and fading to a minimum. But sometimes I was unable to mail film soon enough, resulting in photographs so faded as to be completely different from the originals.

As for my cameras, after day upon day of heat and sand, their condition soon deteriorated. Sand inevitably found its way inside the lenses, making them very sticky, and loud grating noises came forth whenever I focused the cameras. One of the cameras I had overhauled after returning to Japan was completely covered with a film of sand inside. Various other problems arose, such as malfunctioning film counters, but fortunately I was never prevented from taking pictures.

An accident that I would have thought impossible befell one of my telephoto lenses. After the vibrations caused by many days of travel on bad roads, the screws that held the helicoid to the lens itself came loose and fell out, and the lens components actually fell apart. Even so, I continued to get wonderfully sharp pictures by holding the parts together when taking a picture.

During my several trips through the Sahara I used various cameras, ranging from 35 mm to 4 × 5. The ones I used most frequently were the 35 mm and 6 × 7 cameras that I took with me on my first trip. In that overwhelming heat, to carry even *one* kilogram less weight was a help. Here are the main cameras and lenses that I used:

Nikon F (2 bodies) and Nikon F2 Photomic (2 bodies) with these Auto-Nikkon lenses: 20 mm f3.5; 28 mm f3.5; 35 mm f2; 50 mm f1.4; 135 mm f2.8; 200 mm f4; 300 mm f4.5.

Asahi Pentax 6 × 7 with these Super-Takumar lenses: 55 mm f3.5; 75 mm f4.5; 105 mm f2.4; 200 mm f4.

For film, I used Kodachrome X and Kodachrome II in the 35 mm camera and Fujichrome R-100 and Ektachrome X in the 6 × 7. For black and white film, I used Kodak's Tri-X and Plus X. For the photos of the wall paintings in the Tassili-n-Ajjer I used a Lindhof-Technika 4 × 5 camera with Fujichrome and Ektachrome sheet film.

I didn't use any filters to try to get special color effects, but when photographing landscapes I generally used an ultraviolet filter; by taking out a little of the diffused reflections of the sand I was able to get true colors.

Kazuyoshi Nomachi

SAHARA

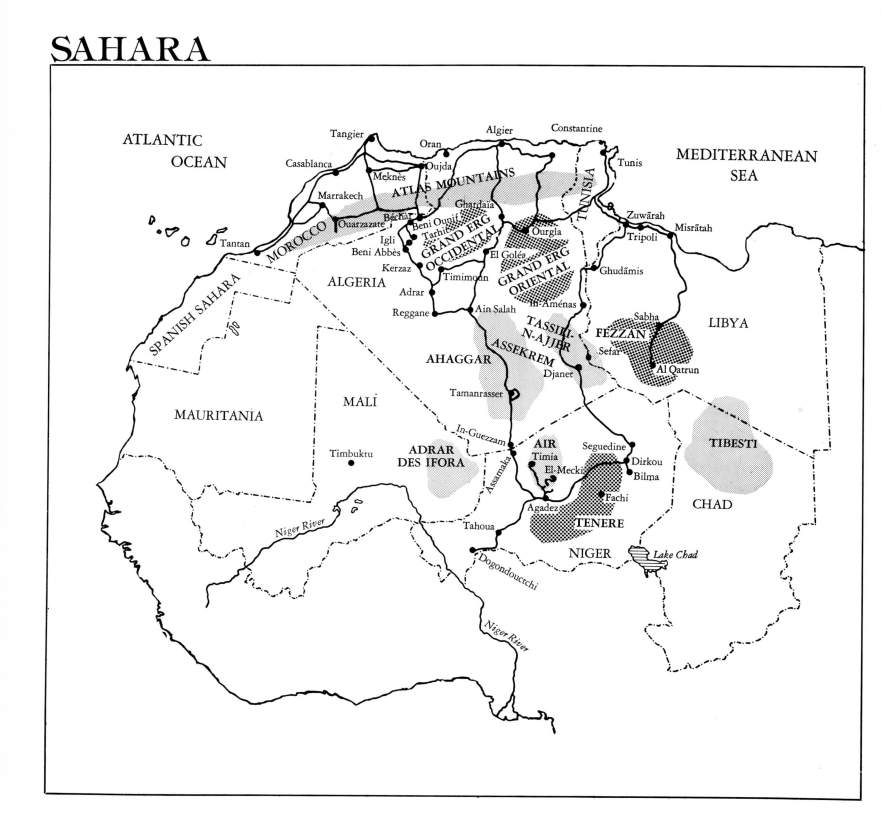

INTRODUCTION

The Desert and Its People

The term *sahara* derives from an Arabic word that originally meant, simply, "a desert." Then at some point it came to be used as a proper noun, designating the vast wasteland of North Africa from the Atlantic Ocean on the west to the Red Sea on the east and, excepting a narrow coastal strip at the northeast, from the Mediterranean southward to the Sudan or to a latitude of about 15 degrees north of the equator. It measures 3,200 miles (5,000 kilometers) from west to east and about 1,000 miles (1,600 kilometers) from north to south, giving it an area of some 3.2 million square miles (9 million square kilometers) — or about one-third of the area of the entire African continent. Of all the deserts on earth, the Sahara is the largest and by far the driest. It well deserves the distinction of being called simply Sahara, "The Desert."

In prehistoric times, during the same climatic changes that brought a series of glacial periods to Europe and other northern regions, the area we now call the Sahara alternated between humid and arid periods. Seven or eight thousand years ago it was the home of the hippopotamus and the elephant. But, beginning about 2000 B.C., its most recent humid period began to give way again to dryness and, by the time of the Christian era, it had become almost as we know it today. Once the drying had started, the topography of North Africa itself hastened the process. The Sahara area consists of vast lowlands in the interior, cut off from the seas by mountainous zones. Hence moisture-laden winds from the seas are walled off from the interior of the continent, and life-giving rains seldom come over the mountains.

Entering the Algerian Sahara by the road through the Atlas Mountains, one sees conditions at a glance. The northern slopes of the mountains, which enjoy a Mediterranean climate, are thickly covered with green trees; but at the top, the green suddenly gives way to the reddish-brown bare wasteland of the southern slopes. Even the few small streams that are fed by rains in the mountains and then flow to the south quickly disappear without a trace as soon as they reach the Sahara, sucked dry by the sandy soil.

In the central regions there are mountainous massifs where great areas of bedrock are exposed to the burning sun, such as the Ahaggar and Tassili-n-Ajjer regions of Algeria, the Adrar des Iforas of Mali, the Aïr of Niger, and the Tibasti of northern Chad. These mountain areas used to have a little rain, and the resulting sparse vegetation made them barely habitable for a few nomads, but even these rains have ceased in recent times and the areas are now all but lifeless.

Despite this, a few nomads stubbornly remain in the midst of this desolation, somehow managing to survive by raising a few goats and camels on the rocky land. The lives of the nomads of the

Ahaggar or the Tassili, for example, seem to have been reduced to bare essentials, as are those of the few plants that struggle to grow here. And towering above all are the windswept peaks of stone, exposed to the full brunt of the violently eroding winds; these are the very outlines of the naked earth, an earth burned completely black, which can only be described as the geography of hell itself.

Below the mountain regions, at an altitude about 1,000 to 1,300 feet (300 to 400 meters) above sea level, stretch the vast gravelly plains. These were formed in ages past by the heavy rains that beat down upon the mountains, washing away bits of stone and depositing them here. Such plains occupy about half the total area of the Sahara.

Beyond the gravel plains are the sand-dune regions. These have been formed by the particles of sand that have eroded from the rocks of the mountains and the gravels of the plains. Ground ever finer and finer, first by the waters and more recently by the raging winds, they have piled up at the edges of the plains. These undulating sand dunes seem to continue endlessly to the distant horizons and actually comprise about twenty percent of the area of the Sahara. They represent the last of the several stages of wind erosion.

In this vast barren land, equal in size to the whole of the United States, two or three million people are said to be living, most of whom are called Berbers. This is not the original name of these peoples but an epithet, meaning "barbarian" or "foreigner," applied to all the peoples found in this region by the Arabs when they invaded it from the east in the seventh century. Hence, Berber is not the name of any specific race or tribe.

One theory holds that the Berbers can be divided into eleven distinct tribal groups, but except for two or three tribes that show distinct characteristics, an outsider cannot distinguish among them easily. Within the permanent settlements around larger oases, Berbers, Arabs, and blacks live together without discrimination, and there is much mixing of blood.

But the nomads preserve their tribal identities. Relations between the tribes used to consist almost exclusively of hostilities, and even today the nomads are very suspicious of all persons outside their own tribe. Hence they live their wandering lives almost entirely alone, having only rare contact with the nomads of other tribes. Some of the main tribal groups of the nomads are the Shaamba, said to be descended from the Arabs, in northeastern Algeria where there is much grazing land; the Regeibat, who spread from southern Morocco to western Algeria; the Maure of Mauritania; the Tuareg, in the central Sahara; and Toubou, in the Tibesti.

Except for the Arabic Shaamba, all the other inhabitants belong to small tribes and are generally called Berbers, and some even include the Shaamba among them. In short, the ethnic origins of the Berbers remain shrouded in mystery, and it is most difficult to classify them by tribes.

To complicate the matter still further, there are also the inhabitants of the Sudan, the generic name for the savanna region of the southern Sahara, extending eastward from Mali through Niger and Chad into the Sudanese Republic. These include various negroid peoples, agricultural tribes from East Africa, and other nomad groups. All in all, the Sahara and its environs appear to be a sort of racial melting pot.

The Oases

Oasis — what a gentle ring the word has. One immediately imagines a green island appearing miraculously in the desert and an ever-flowing spring amid fresh, lush verdure. This picture describes well enough the appearance of a Saharan oasis when seen from a distance. But when one actually sets foot in the oasis, what had seemed so verdant from afar turns out to be nothing but the dusty green of spiny, drought-resistant date palms. And as for the spring that never runs dry, the water one draws up with great effort from the deep wells is muddy and full of sand. It is not long before we realize that the oasis image that we hold so dear is not to be found here. It exists only in the imaginations of those who have never seen the desert.

No matter how faded the green seems to us, for the people who live in the desert the oasis is the source of life, the refuge that supports their very existence. It is a special place that has been developed for cultivation in the middle of the inhospitable Sahara. It is a place that people have somehow managed to make arable in the face of crushingly adverse conditions, a place that generation after generation has struggled to preserve from the inroads of the desert. Under the date palms watered by man, in their shade, protecting the land from sand and scorching sun, life-giving seeds somehow have been nurtured.

I have described the Saharan oasis in general, but depending upon its location and inhabitants, an oasis may vary in its appearance. Let me tell you about the oasis of Igli, a small Saharan village in western Algeria where we spent some time.

Like most other oases, Igli, which has a population of about two thousand, permits almost no economic activity except small-scale oasis farming — and not enough of that to support all the people. Hence, many of the men leave to take jobs in the cities to the north, and the population of the village is reduced by about half for most of each year. The only people a visitor sees are children and old men, since the women stay in their houses and rarely walk outside. About eighty percent of the inhabitants are Shluh, one of the important Berber tribes; the rest are either black Haratins or Arabs.

The village consists of a central mosque enclosed within high walls and surrounded by the older houses called *ksar*, which look like thickly clustered beehives. Beyond these are the more recent houses, built of concrete or mud. All of this is squeezed into an area of at most one square kilometer. Although the desert is vast, the areas where life can be sustained are extremely limited, and the population density of oases such as Igli is as high as that of a big city. People live crowded together because conditions in the desert are so harsh that no single family or individual could ever face nature there alone.

In the lawless days of old, each *ksar* was surrounded by a high wall for protecton against desert robbers. Villages were not designed for hospitality to strangers, and even today there is an almost palpable feeling of hostility when strangers enter the village. The style of architecture provides protection not only against people but also against sun and sand. Viewed from a low hill nearby, the village nestles cozily like a pile of flotsam that has been washed up by the waves of sand dunes behind it. The physical appearance of the oasis also reveals the important position religion occupies in the life of the people: the whiteness of the mosque's minaret, with loudspeakers attached on all four sides, towers conspicuously above the low reddish-brown houses of sun-baked brick.

Inside its thick outer walls of mud, a house consists of a number of small separate rooms built around an inner garden. Each room has a single door opening onto the courtyard and one small window for light. Entering one of these dim, cool rooms, one feels a sense of relief at escaping from the strong, dizzying light of the street and from the constant threat of sandstorms. Despite the darkness of the rooms, they are completely dry; there is practically no humidity.

Within the room, every inch of space on the walls is covered with posters and pinups and other pictures in what seemed to us an excess of enthusiasm. It was as if the occupants were determined to fill all the available space. To them, a blank expanse of wall signified emptiness, like the monotonously empty desert that surrounded the oasis.

Another thing that struck us as strange was the people's custom of locking things up. Every time anyone opened and closed something, be it the wooden front door, the door of the guest room, the closet for European clothing, a small chest, or even a desk drawer, he or she first had to unlock and then relock it. Surely the contents were not so valuable, and with family bonds strong between them, why were they so fearful? Shutting themselves in, completely apart from the outside world, is perhaps natural for a people who are fighting to survive a fierce environment. I suppose that, without even realizing it, the people carry this habit of protecting themselves from the outside world into their family life as well.

On the western edge of the village, along the Saoura watercourse, are the groves of thickly clustered date palms and the farms of the oasis. Date palms originally grew wild here because the area was rich in underground water. The people dug wells in the shade of the trees and later planted still more palm trees. Gradually tillable soil developed, and farmland came into being. The small-scale farming that thus became possible created the oasis culture. This culture is so closely tied to the date palm that it could also be called a date-palm culture.

Trees are so few in the desert that every part of them is a treasure. The fruit of the date palm provides an essential food, and its trunk and leaves are widely used in various ways essential to life. The dates, bursting with sweetness, are harvested once a year, with a single tree yielding an average of about 110 pounds (50 kilograms) of fruit. Today, when it is possible to get various foods from outside, dates are eaten mainly for dessert, but in the past they were one of the most valuable staple foods. The palm trunks have long been indispensable as building materials, serving as rafters set into walls made of sun-dried bricks covered with mud plaster. These fibrous trunks are also used to make various implements such as the poles for the lever-type wells, the well curbs, and mortars and pestles. As for the palm leaves, their uses are endless — as fences to keep sand from blowing in, for roof thatching, making baskets, hats, and other handcrafted items, as well as for fuel.

Oasis farming also is conducted in an extremely intensive way. For example, the water that makes possible the growth of the trees and agricultural products has to be drawn from deep wells. Although power pumps are increasingly used in a few regions, water for the most part is still raised to the surface just as it was centuries ago, by drawing up buckets from wells ten to thirty meters deep, using human or animal power. This must be done daily without fail, and it is no easy matter. Wherever there is the slightest shade, vegetables are planted to fight evaporation of moisture, even on the sides of the small ditches that carry water from the wells to the fields. Constant vigilance is needed: if the people relax their guard even a little, in no time the land will return to its former sandy state.

The Tuareg People

The Tuareg, among whom we spent some time, are the most aggressive and unfriendly of all the Berber tribes. A nomadic people with comparatively light skin, they live in the central mountainous region of the Sahara, where conditions are at their harshest. For several centuries the Tuareg controlled the trade routes of the Sahara, amassing much wealth and thus dominating the entire desert. Unable to resist the wave of change, however, they have been reduced to making a bare living as farmers and nomads, living for the most part in mountain areas such as Ahaggar and Tassili-n-Ajjer in Algeria, Aïr in Niger, and Adrar des Iforas in Mali. They have an alphabet in the *tifinar* script, which is almost ideographic, similar to old Libyan or Hamitic writing, and said to be derived from ancient Phoenician. Among themselves they speak a language called Tamashek. Although the Tuareg are nominally Moslem, their women go unveiled. The men, however, maintain the old habit of extreme unfriendlinesss to strangers, as can be seen by their custom of covering their faces completely with a long veil, leaving only their eyes exposed.

The Tuareg also wrap their heads with an extremely long turban to protect themselves from sun and sand, but this custom is common to all desert tribes. The veil of the Tuareg men, however, is stubbornly maintained for other than practical reasons. According to one explanation, they believe that if one exposes one's face in front of a stranger, evil spirits will invade the body through the nose and mouth. In former times the veil was not removed even while eating; instead, it was lifted with the left hand while food was brought to the mouth with the right. Today, however, this custom has all but disappeared, and most people eat and drink with the veils slipped down under their chins. Also, friends stand chatting on any street corner of a village with their veils slipped down, but whenever an outsider comes near them, they quickly pull their veils up and stare at the intruder with sharp, suspicious eyes.

The Tuareg carry a sword with a thirty-six-inch blade at the hip, and over their heavy clothes a flowing, ankle-length robe called a *gandoura* flutters in the wind. Their sandals are made of a special leather, and they seem to glide as they stride across the sand. Altogether, they look exactly like our romantic image of desert sheiks.

The Tuareg are often called "the blue men." Their favorite cloth is dyed an indigo color that ranges from deep blue to blue-black and acts much like carbon paper: when the cloth is rubbed, the blue color comes off on the skin. Since both men and women use this cloth for many different items of clothing — the men's turbans, veils, and *gandoura,* and the women's shawls and robes — this blue color becomes a kind of face paint and produces the impression that their skin is blue.

The Tuareg are also a deeply superstitious people and carry small amulets wherever they go. These are in the form of small leather pouches that are hung from the neck or fastened to the arms. Inside the pouches are slips of paper on which are written verses from the Koran or magic spells.

One often gets the feeling that the Tuareg are a completely idle and unproductive people. This is probably the result of the long history of the Tuareg in the Sahara. Until they were driven from their homes during the Arab invasion of Africa that began in the seventh century, they dominated the Sahara and made great profits by providing safe passage along the caravan routes. At that time their capital was at Germa (today's

Jarmah) in Fezzan, but some say that later the capital was located in the Ahaggar. Perhaps this was because the Tuareg were pushed as far back as the mountainous region of the central Sahara by the invading Arabs. But even so, as "desert raiders," they continued to control most of the Sahara for several more centuries, supporting themselves by dealing in slaves captured from the Sudan savanna region (keeping some to do their own manual labor) and by raiding the Saharan oases, until they were finally subdued by the French at the turn of this century.

We once had the opportunity of seeing a procession of proud Tuareg warriors riding camels at a festival at Agadez in Niger. There were more than a hundred of them, carrying spears and swords, their faces wrapped in veils, and they made an overwhelming sight. When we saw their sword dance at the Algerian Independence Day festival held at Djanet, we were forcibly reminded of how much the volatile beauty of this people arose from their love of fighting. Accompanied by drums and the singing of women, several men, each carrying a sword, appeared dressed in indigo veils and *gandoura* and scarlet sashes. As they moved through the gathering twilight, gliding on noiseless feet in a crouching, ready position, their figures were expressive of the intense, choking tension of the desert itself.

Moving south from the center of the Algerian Sahara, one finds more and more of the negroid agricultural people called the Haratin, said to be descendants of slaves brought here from the Sudan by the Tuareg. Even now, Tuareg society preserves a strict status system, with three distinct classes — the nobles, who were the warriors of old; the family retainers or stewards, who take care of the nobles' animals; and the Haratin, who work hard at farming the oases. But now that the nobles can no longer engage in their principal activity of raiding and plundering, these class distinctions are gradually disappearing.

The Tuareg were originally a Mediterranean people who invaded the Sahara from the north and are said to have carried out a military campaign in Europe. Now they are becoming more and more racially mixed with negroid peoples; and, especially among those who have settled in the Aïr region in the south and have become agricultural people themselves, the original whiteness of the Tuareg skin has all but disappeared. The nomadic Tuareg in the northern regions of Ahaggar and Tassili, however, have largely maintained the purity of their blood.

The Tuareg in the south — even those who have remained nomads rather than settling down to agriculture — have been greatly influenced by their agricultural neighbors and other nomadic tribes of the region; as a result they have lost much of their fierceness and become somewhat freer in their manners and customs. In contrast, the Tuareg in the more northern regions, leading nomadic lives in the isolated mountainous zones, with almost no contact with other tribes, have maintained their xenophobic character. Because of their deep suspicion of strangers and of the outside world in general, until quite recently they had no formal system of education and hence had been left behind by the wave of modernization that has been advancing, slowly but surely over the Sahara. On the other hand, their former slaves, the Haratin — who have become settled, agricultural people — have benefited from education, and many are now actively participating in the government. Thus one can say that the relative social positions of the two peoples, formerly masters and slaves, have, in effect, been reversed.

Even when compared to that of other nomads, the life of the Tuareg of the mountain regions is particularly miserable. They suffer from a chronic lack of protein in their diet, and — living in areas with so little water — they lack even rudimentary concepts of hygiene. Eye and skin diseases are common. Their customary hostility to outsiders acts as a destructive force by encouraging marriage to close relatives, with a resulting high incidence of abnormality among their offspring. Hence, their brave ways and tremendous life force nothwithstanding, as long as they continue their nomadic life in the mountains where there is nothing but stones, the Tuareg face an increasingly black future.

The Tassili-n-Ajjer Plateau

The Tassili-n-Ajjer of southern Algeria belies its name. In the Tamashek language of the Tuareg the term means a plateau with a river running through it. In actuality, the region is a wilderness with an average altitude of 3,200 feet (1,000 meters) or more above sea level, making it resemble a range of mountains rather than a gentle plateau. It spreads across the center of the Sahara for approximately 30 to 40 miles (50 to 60 kilometers) from east to west and about 500 miles

(800 kilometers) from north to south. Its many strange sandstone formations are greatly eroded and from a distance resemble the ruins of ancient cities. There are weird clumps of boulders that look like temple towers, and spires of sandstone that appear to be fantastic forests. Other formations look as if the entrails of some giant animal had been spread out over the earth to dry in the scorching sun. This terrain, so strange as to seem to be another world, was created long ago by the irrestible force of water erosion.

The Sahara was once green and fertile and, several thousand years ago, supported a flourishing civilization. People lived in the shadows of rocks whose bases had been deeply gouged out by swirling waters, and over the years they recorded their lives on the surfaces of countless rock walls. These wall paintings continued to be made over a period of several thousand years, and they show a variety of styles. The earliest scenes were of hunting, dancing, and worship. Later, the cattle-raising people who flowed into the area painted many pictures of cows, and their depictions of festivals vividly reflect an Egyptian influence.

Thus it was that countless pictures were painted of the peaceful life of several thousand years blessed by good climatic conditions. But then, by about the year 2000 B.C., the Sahara gradually started to dry up. As the land grew arid and conditions of survival inexorably changed, painting techniques too began to deteriorate. By about the beginning of the Christian era, the ancestors of the present-day Tuareg are said to have appeared with camels on this desert plateau, which had been abandoned by the hunting and cattle-raising peoples who painted the pictures.

Imagine a green Sahara! Logic says this was not impossible, considering that Europe was once covered by glaciers. And to anyone who knows the arid Sahara of present times, the thought of greenery covering this wasteland adds another dimension to the present reality.

To think that this vast dead expanse of sand and gravel was a fertile land until only a few thousand years ago; to think that people who lived here were blessed with ample rainfall! This land has been transformed so completely, so cruelly, that now—except for the occasional oases—there is no cranny in which the smallest seed can sprout. It is a sobering thought, and one that is all but unbelievable.

And yet here in the mountains of the Tassili, the rare and unmistakable power of pictorial expression granted to human beings has been exercised in a number of wall paintings offering visible proof of a green Sahara, a verdant land whose faint perfume reaches us across several thousand years. These wall paintings are generally classified chronologically in the following periods (the dates are of course, approximate): 1) 5000–3500 B.C. when the inhabitants were a hunting people; 2) 3500–2000 B.C., cattle raisers; 3) 2000–300 B.C., horse raisers; and 4) 300 B.C.–A.D. 400, camel raisers. Most of the innumerable paintings have been badly weathered over the centuries. But a few dozen have escaped the ravages of time and are in almost perfect condition, ready to tell us much about life in those distant days. These paintings are from the cattle-raisers period and were painted with a particular sense of design.

When I stood in front of these paintings, a strange and deep emotion welled up within me. It was completely different from anything the Sahara had ever produced in me—something that was awakened for the first time. The feeling came from the soft, dewy harmony of the pictures, from their echo of a green world filled to overflowing with the water I had known in my life back home, the moisture that suddenly filled me with such nostalgia. The feeling was intensified by the fact that the pictures were emitting the aura of an impossible past, here in this still wasteland enclosed by fantastically eroded sandstone formations.

How had I come to this spot in the Sahara? Certainly there had been difficulties. It had taken half a day of hard climbing up a steep, rugged gravel slope, at an altitude of more than 3,400 feet (1,000 meters), to reach this point. And before that? But that's another story. . . .

SAHARA

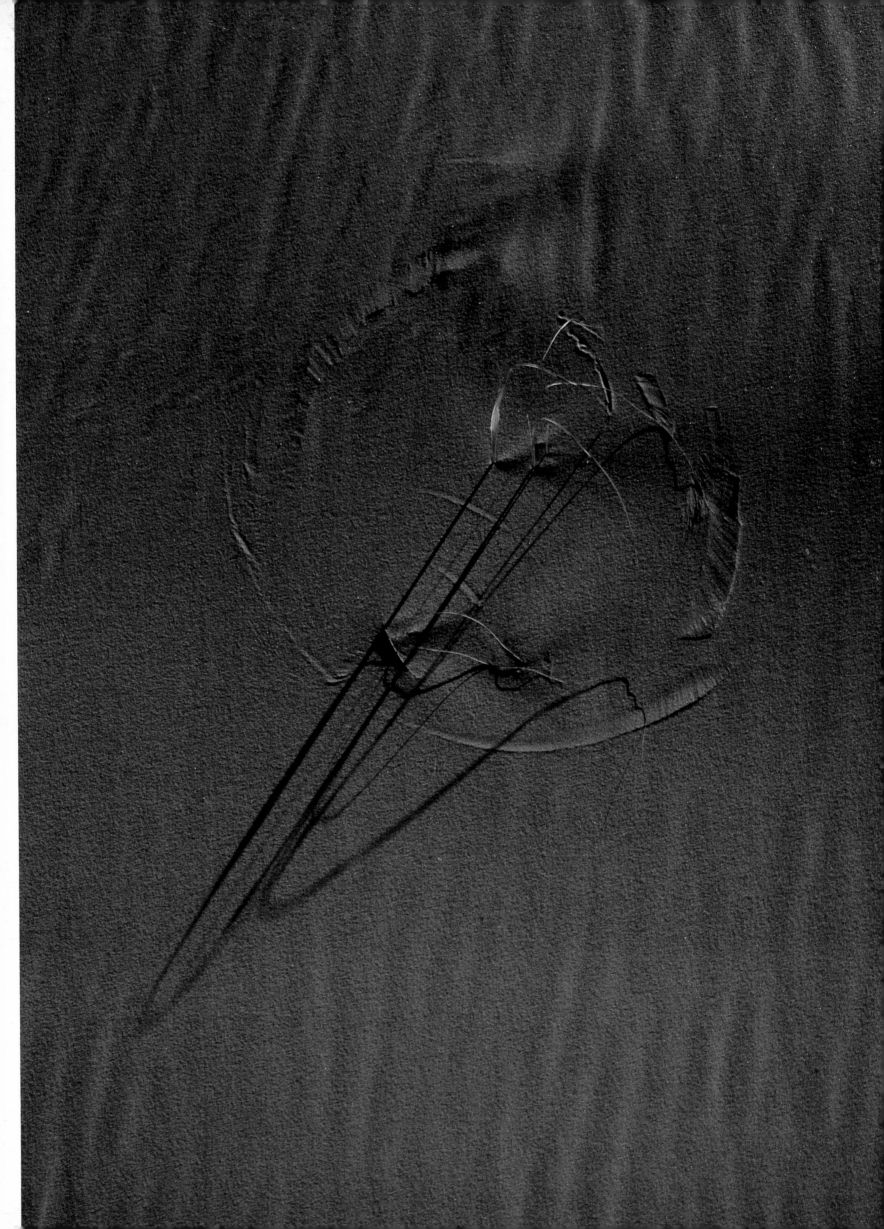

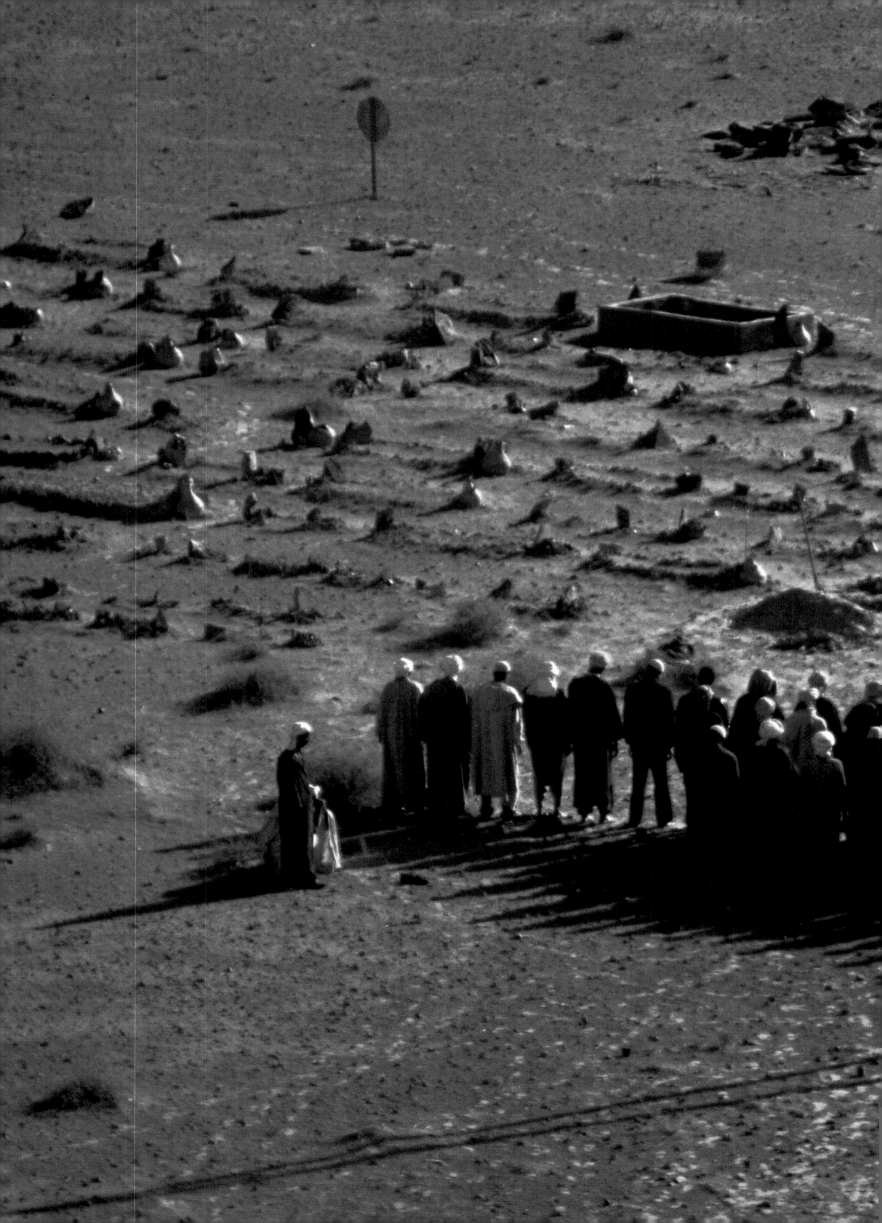

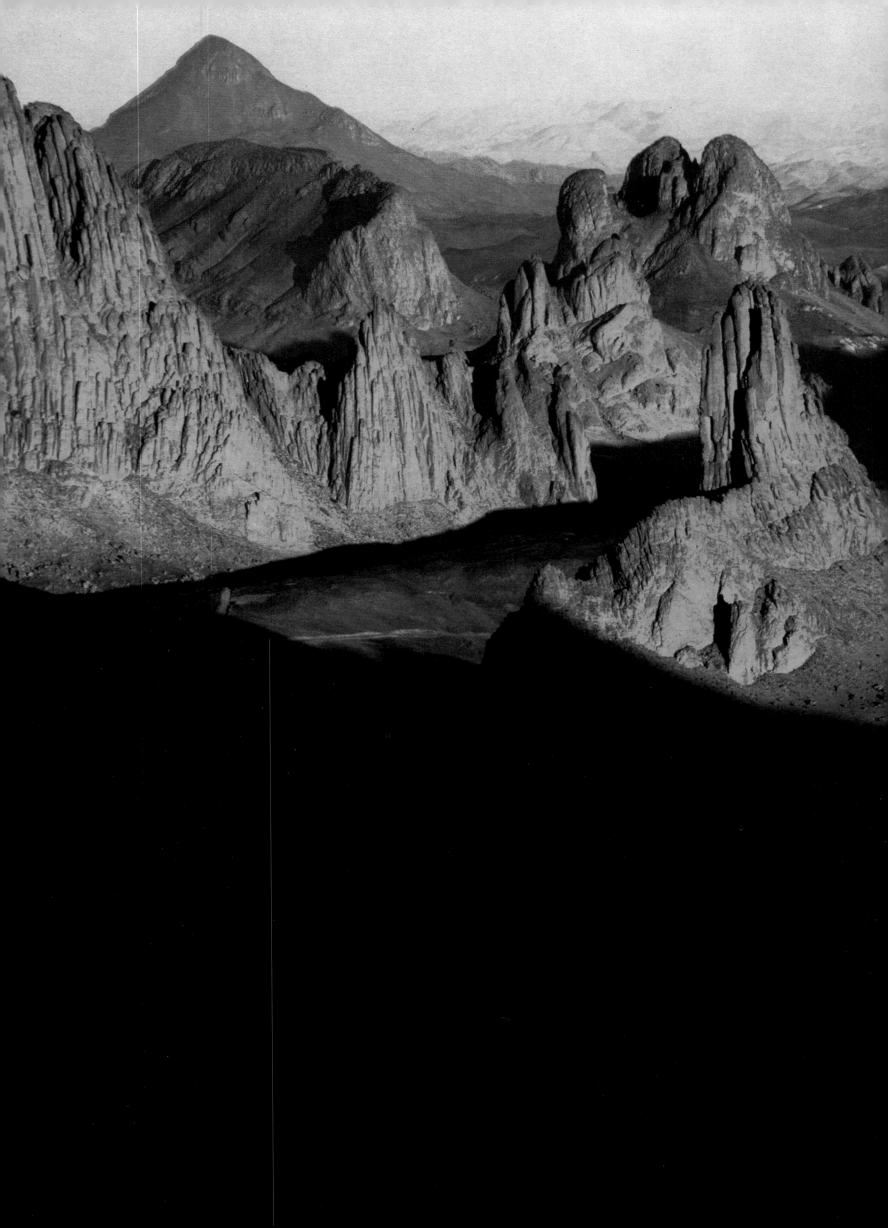

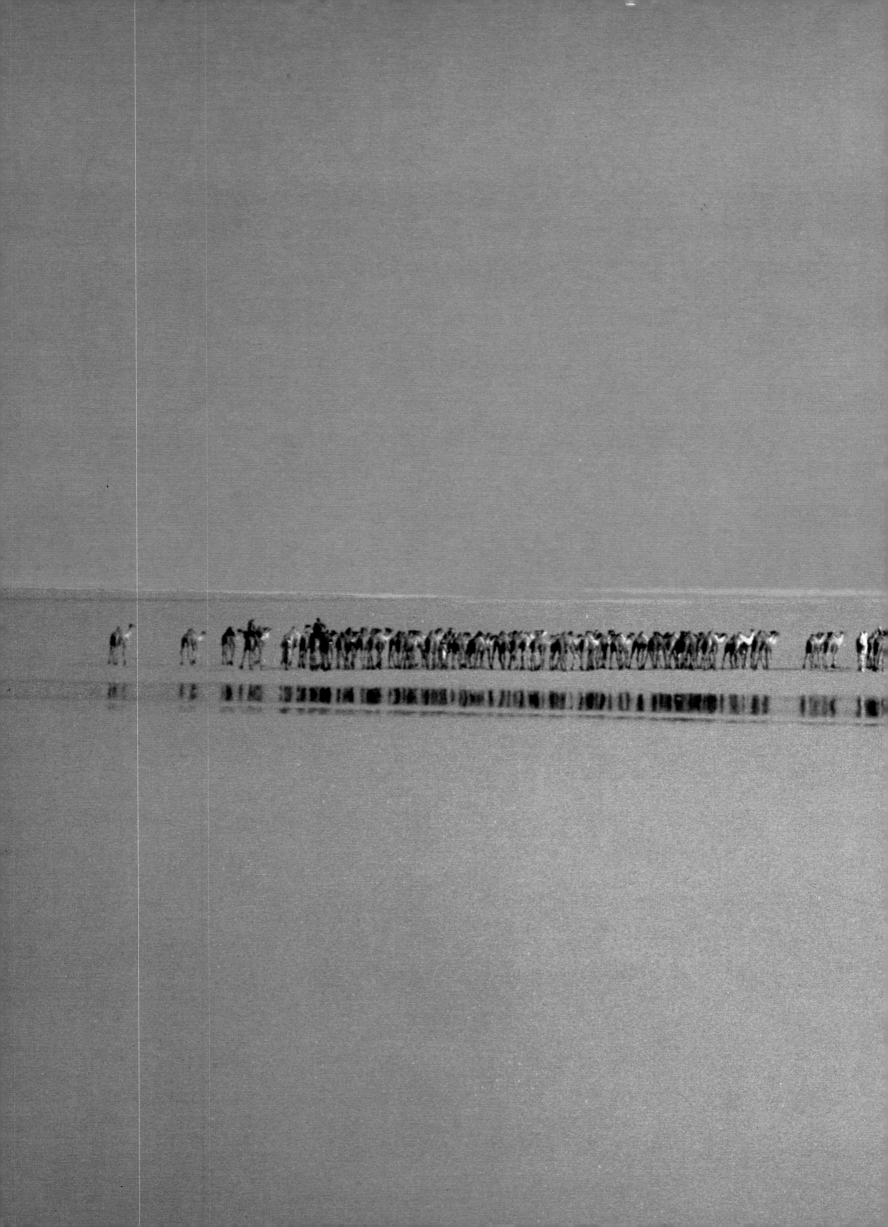

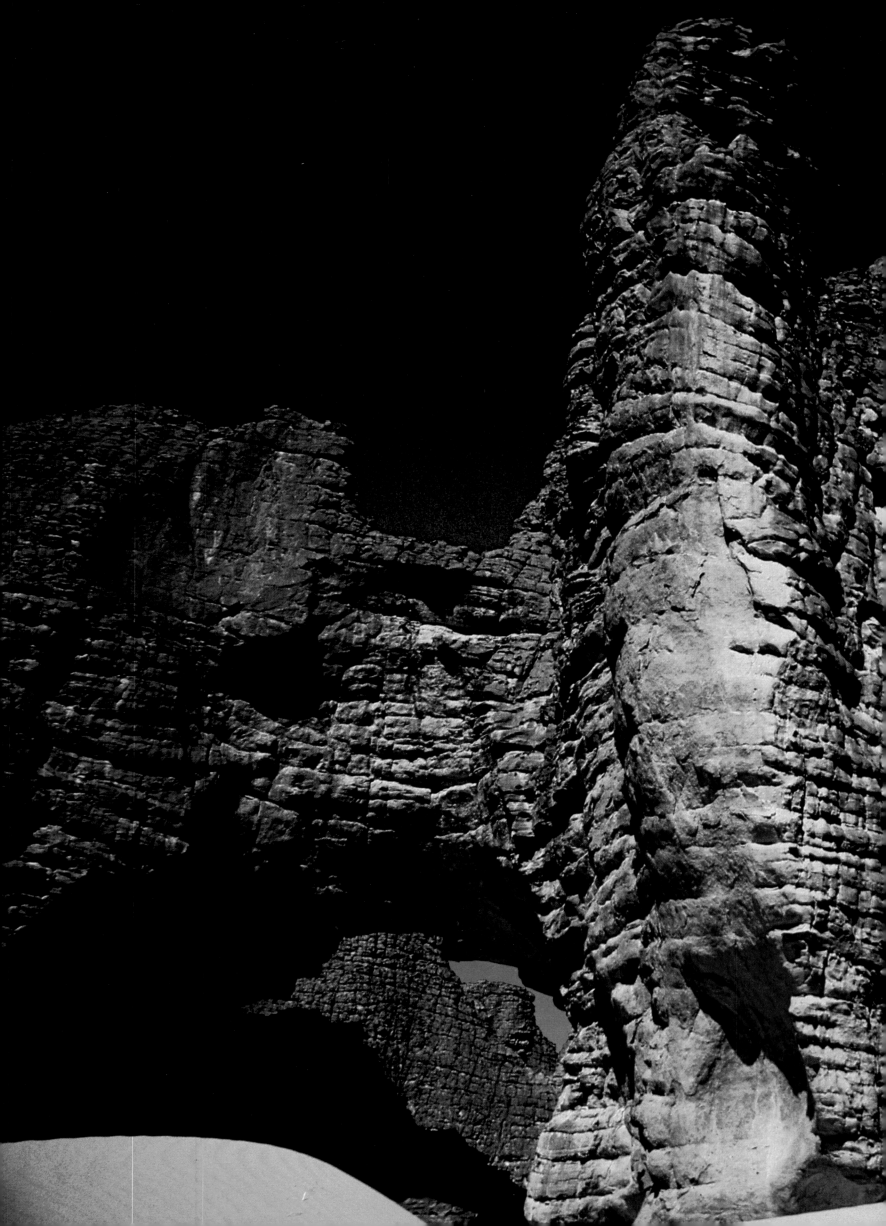

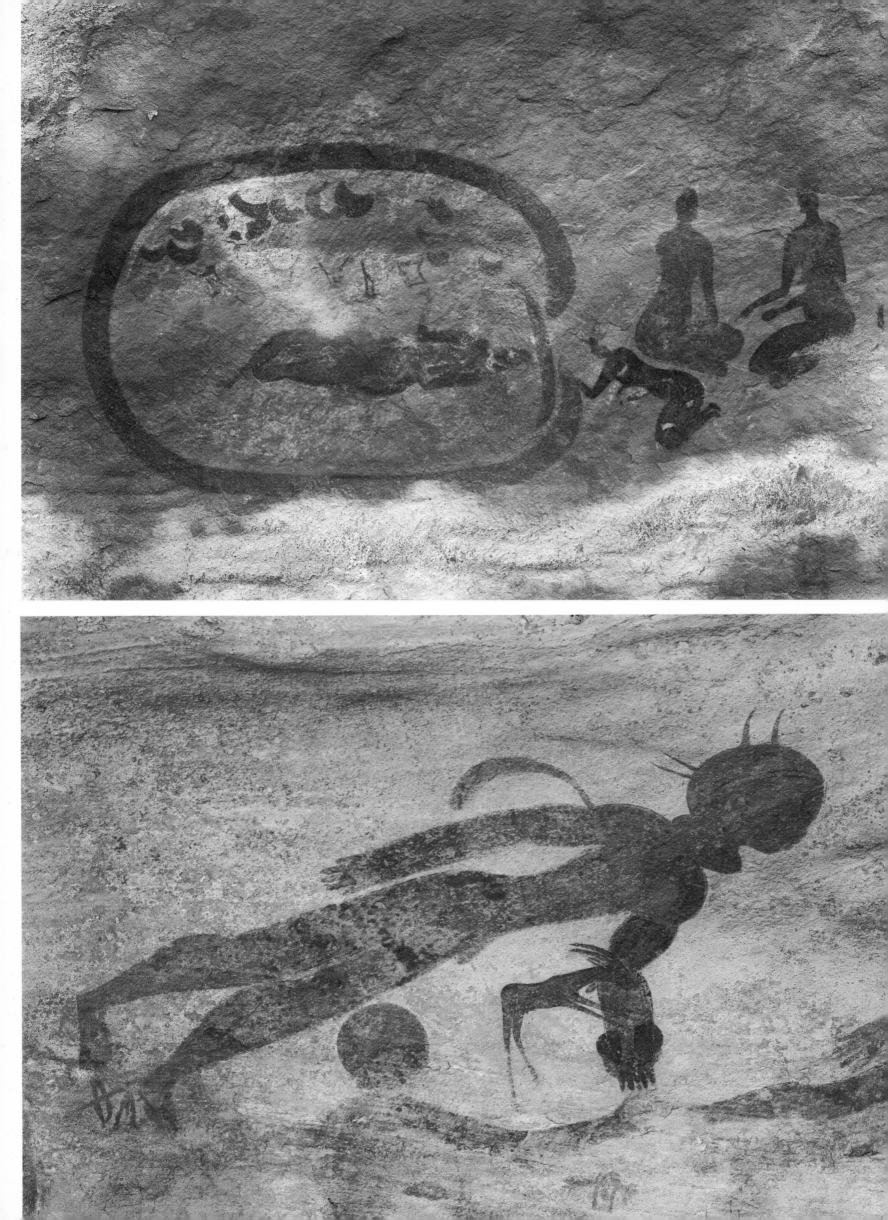

SAHARA DIARIES

To the Sahara

The rays of the sun were almost stinging, and the asphalt road stretched out in a straight line across the monotonous gravelly plain that seemed to continue on and on to the ends of the earth. The desert that spread out to the horizon on either side of the road was an expanse of stillness and sterility suggestive of the ghastly aftermath of some ancient holocaust.

After a time — was it minutes or hours since we had descended the foothills of the Atlas Mountains? — the road described a wide curve as it started up a steep incline. At the top my field of vision suddenly expanded and light brown sand dunes abruptly leaped into sight. I gasped. How could anyone have imagined that that endless rocky plain would suddenly change to this undulating expanse of sand dunes?

I stopped the car and was taking photographs almost before I realized it. And what was that over there? Looking closely, I thought I saw a cluster of mud houses and green date palms huddled at the foot of a group of sand dunes almost 320 feet (100 meters) high.

It was the Tarhit Oasis. And again, wasn't this a strange combination — the green of the date palms contrasting with the endless undulations of brown sand. Above everything was the heavy weight of the deep blue sky. Within all this emptiness, just where the brown and the green and the blue contrast was strongest, there appeared signs of human life. For me it was a moment of revelation, as though the desert had cast away one of its veils of mystery.

This was my first sight of the Sahara. It was February, 1972, and my friend Izukura and I were driving an old secondhand car we had acquired in Paris. We had made our way about 55 miles (90 kilometers) south from the Béchar gateway into the Algerian Sahara.

We circled the oasis and continued on southward along the rough track that skirted the sand dunes, thinking this would be the shortest way to the Igli Oasis. But soon the car was stuck in the sand. Some children came out of a grove of date palms and helped us push the car out. We had clearly underestimated the dangers of that route but soon we were on our way back along the road we had come by.

It was at this moment that the Sahara removed another veil. Suddenly, black clouds covered the sky that a moment before had been so piercingly blue, and without further warning, we were engulfed by a violent sand storm, which quickly changed to a mixture of sand and rain. Within a second we could no longer see more than a few feet ahead. Stopping the car in the midst of the raging hot wind, we closed the windows tightly and sat helpless, staring out into the storm. The wind came in great gusts, with a shrill sound, and made our car shake and rattle violently.

Izukura was in the driver's seat, and I wonder what he was thinking as we sat there. Suddenly a gust of wind seemed to come right into the car: Izukura had opened a door and jumped out onto the sand. Standing in the wind, he looked for all the world as if he were dancing. We were dressed for the desert in long hooded robes, which we had bought in Morocco, and his was flapping behind him as he abandoned himself to the wind, waving his arms and legs. Suddenly he was caught by the wind, which pushed him rapidly along before it toward the crest of the slope on which we had stopped.

I somehow felt that I, too, must dance madly in the wind, and I joined Izukura on the slope. At the top, the softness of billowing sand suddenly appeared before us again, and in a flash we were exposed to the tremendous full force of sand and wind. It was an incoherent, unfathomable force, such as I had never felt before. Somehow the body is overcome by an impulse to surrender entirely to it. And there we stood, while the sensual curves of the sand dunes, which just a few minutes before had been inert weights upon the earth, were flinging themselves into the wind with a roaring sound as though a blaze were being fanned higher and higher.

And within a few more minutes — the storm could not have lasted more than a half-hour — it was all over. The wind and the rain stopped completely, and it was as if they had never been.

* * *

Two days later, after the sun had set, we were driving north again after having reached our southernmost destination, Adrar. Now as we drove through the desert night we were filled with strange feelings. The wide world around us was only barely visible in the moonlight: all we could see were the twenty or thirty meters of black asphalt road that were lit by our headlights. Both of us were on the edge of exhaustion — the strain of our tight schedule was beginning to tell — but perhaps for that very reason our perceptions were all the more sharply honed. I can't remember which one of us was actually driving, but we both had our eyes riveted upon the cone of brightness that our headlights made ahead of us. We seemed to be trying to relieve the strain by shifting our hands and feet and gripping the steering wheel or door handles tightly.

The car was climbing a long, steep incline. Reaching the top, we again had the strange experience of seeing a great mountain of sand occupying our suddenly expanded field of vision. Everything was in deep shadow except that great

dune which gleamed eerily in the moonlight. Spontaneously we decided to camp there at the base of the sand dune. In the limitless expanse of land covered with rocks and stones, that place alone looked as if it were gently inviting us. Leaving the road, we drove carefully through the soft sand to the dune, and when we turned off the engine we couldn't hear anything at all except the ringing in our ears.

Somehow in this great open space we felt strangely calm and protected. The dune, even higher than we had thought, curved around behind us, almost as if it were a protective screen between us and limitless space. The moonlight was a clear, shiny white, but the sand that received its rays was a gleaming deep brown color, and all around us the cold night spread its absolute stillness. The surface of the sand that had been baking in the sun all day was already turning cold, but when I dug down into it with my hands I discovered that the sand below was still slightly warm. Wrapped in blankets, we sat on the sand and drank up the little bit of sake we somehow still had.

The desert at night presents an entirely different face. No longer does the sun beat down on one's head, no longer are there violent sand storms. The desert is a place of extremes, with no gradations, no middle point. We spent the night inside the cramped car.

Next morning, we woke with the sun and started to climb the dune that had stood sentinel for us during the long night. We climbed intently, sinking up to our ankles in the soft sand. It was very rough going and our hearts were beating as though they would burst, but we kept on climbing.

Finally we were standing at the top. The view was magnificent. The undulation of sand dunes that extended beyond the farthest horizon was breathtaking. Now the dunes seemed steeped in moisture, and in the light of the early morning sun they were not brown but gleamed like tarnished silver.

1973

The next time I went to the Sahara was the following year, in 1973. My wife and I rented a car in Europe and traveled around the northern Sahara for a little more than two months.

As we grew accustomed to the desert, we began to understand something of the lives of the people. To know a people, it is not enough simply to see the land on which they live, the shifting sand dunes or the rugged mountains. We had to see how deeply the life of the people was rooted in this land, to come to know the rich range of their facial expressions, to understand that, even if they were not blessed with material comforts and had to live under overwhelmingly adverse conditions, they actually enjoyed an idyllic way of life.

The faces of the old people were particularly smooth and serene. Watching a group of tall old men, staffs in hand, their bodies enveloped in white robes, quietly enjoying the coolness in the shade of some palm trees, I thought — strange as it may sound — that if paradise were to exist on this earth, it would be right here in the interior of the Sahara, in these silent oases, besieged by the shifting sands. And the deeper one goes into these distant parts of the Sahara, where living conditions are at their harshest, the smoother the faces of the people who live here become. If I were to put it strongly, I would say that the very depth of the silence and barrenness of the Sahara is a necessary condition for its beauty.

October, 1974 — September, 1975

The following year, in October, 1974, I made a third trip into the Sahara, again accompanied by my wife. I had left Japan with the thought that I should like to spend a full year in the Sahara, to know one complete turn of the seasons in order to experience the desert both in heat and in cold. We traveled through the Sahara until September, 1975, using first a Range Rover and then a Land Rover, both sturdy enough for cross-country travel. And then we traveled to the Tassili-n-Ajjer region by plane, staying there another month, thus rounding out my full Saharan year.

Within the Sahara

My wife and I got into our car and set off alone over the soft sand toward the distant horizon. Our feelings were a confused mixture of intoxication and uneasiness, as though, against our wills, we were being pulled toward the fathomless darkness.

We were now deep in the Sahara of the Tuareg. The day after leaving Agadez in Niger, we turned off the gravel road that we had been following northward, and there — spread out before our eyes — was the great sand plain called Ténéré. The prospect was one of deep sand con-

tinuing on to Dirkou, a small oasis about 300 miles (500 kilometers) to the east. Countless half-obliterated automobile ruts stretched out over the sand as if they were being sucked up into the horizon. And that was our road. The great sand plain of Ténéré extends southward as far as Lake Chad, and in the past much of it was part of the lake itself. But now the lake has receded more than 300 miles (500 kilometers) to the south. I was told that at Fachi, a small plateau about 125 miles (200 kilometers) to the east of our campsite on that particular night, a number of shell heaps had been discovered, suggesting that Fachi was once on the shore of the lake.

We started off into the wasteland. After driving for about thirty minutes, we stopped and got out to stretch our legs. Already the mountains behind us were hidden from sight by the curvature of the earth, and there was nothing to be seen in any direction except the unbroken line of the encircling horizon. There was not so much as a cloud in the sky, which was more colorless than blue. And there in the middle of the sky was the sun, shedding its hot rays relentlessly upon this shadowless, ominous silence.

The only clue we had as to our course was the track of ruts left by vehicles that had preceded us yesterday or the day before yesterday or some time in the past. Everyone who travels this route has to set off in the same way into the sea of sand, following these precarious ruts that look as if they will disappear in the first gust of strong wind. They lead away eastward in an absolutely straight line, like rails over the flat and hard sandy earth. But we had no particular trouble in following them. To avoid getting stuck in the sand, we reduced the air pressure of our tires as much as possible, thereby increasing the area of rubber that touched the ground. This also made the car all but free of vibration, producing the sensation of our being in a sailboat gliding across the surface of a placid lake.

But when we came to places where the sand was loose instead of packed hard, we could no longer afford to enjoy a relaxed sail. We had to zigzag frantically back and forth, in search of ground that was even the slightest bit harder. I had to get a good grip on the steering wheel and keep my eyes glued to the ground. Whenever one of the wheels would hit a particularly soft patch of sand, the car would be pulled violently aside, deflected in the direction of that wheel. If we didn't get out of the loose sand immediately, the car would burrow deeper and deeper as the wheels spun uselessly. At such moments we felt as though we had been abandoned by the people whose ruts we were following and who — we imagined — had been able to keep going without mishap. But then, after we extricated ourselves with great difficulty, we would find a place where they had had their own troubles. There would be tire tracks dug deeply into the sand, as if a large truck had been badly stuck, and the footprints of many people who had probably had to climb down and help push the truck out of the sand.

That day we kept driving until late. Then we camped in the sand. It was two days since we had left Agadez. We were encircled by the horizon; night had completely closed in; there was not a sound, not a shape. There were no wind patterns in the sand, no undulations, not even pebbles. There was only the ground itself, spreading out like an endless carpet. If a photographer can bring back any memories of such a spot, what could they be other than a half-moon hanging in the sky and the twinkling of myriad stars?

We started to make a fire in order to prepare our evening meal. Since our cooking gas was low (until we could replenish it at a supply station) we had to save it for times of high winds when we couldn't make an open fire. Naturally, there was no firewood in this barren waste, but we had taken the trouble to gather bunches of thorny dry branches near Agadez and tie them to the roof of the car.

After we had eaten and spread our air mattresses on the sand, I lay thinking about something I had chanced to see by the roadside as we drove along that day. At first glance, it had seemed to be nothing but an ordinary flat stone about the size of a pot cover. But there on the sand-covered waste it looked an utterly strange, alien thing. Stopping to pick it up, I examined it closely. The surface, scoured by the sand, was so polished that it gleamed. And when I looked harder, I saw there was a gentle, round hollow carved on the surface, too deep to have resulted from natural erosion.

If it hadn't been made by the sand, I thought, then perhaps it had been made by man; maybe it was one of the first utensils ever made by our distant ancestors, a stone mortar for grinding grain. Was this conclusion of mine too far-fetched? Not here in the Sahara, where one often finds artifacts lying about, just as they were carelessly abandoned by people who lived here thousands, tens of thousands of years ago when the land was covered with green. The reason is

simple: no one has come along since then to carry the objects away.

Once we amused ourselves by looking for arrowheads in the deep interior of the Algerian Sahara. By just bending over and walking around a bit we found an amazing number of articles — not arrowheads alone. Strewn about on the sand among the small stones were such things as pottery shards and discs made of the shells of ostrich eggs and pierced with a hole for making necklaces. In less than an hour we had made thirty or more such finds.

My mortar stone wasn't a unique object that happened there by chance: when we looked around we found quite a number of similar stones lying where they had fallen, half-buried in the sand. And we found one other strange thing — the shriveled leg of a small bird to which was attached a leg-band engraved with the word "Finland." What a strange juxtaposition — these stone implements, which had probably lain there for several thousands of years, and the remains of a dead trespasser, a North European bird blown into the desert by capricious winds. (I still look at the leg-band wonderingly from time to time!)

Suddenly my reverie was broken by a faint hum and a blurred light on the western horizon. The flickering light and the faint sounds, both growing in intensity as they neared us, seemed to be some phenomenon of nature. But after about ten minutes we were able to distinguish the headlights of four trucks and the sound of roaring engines heading in our direction. As though by reflex, we both jumped up and hurriedly put out our fire. Small animals, startled by the noise and the lights, were scurrying to hide themselves in the sand.

The trucks passed at a point about a kilometer away from us, driving in a straight line across the desert. After they had disappeared, for some reason we breathed a sigh of relief. We felt as though we had successfully protected something as brittle and transparent as a glass sphere, something that had grown in the silence of the desert night, protected it from the violence of light and noise. It was like escaping a night raid by bandits.

Next day, around noon, we reached the well of Achegour. There we found the four trucks that had passed us the night before. For desert travelers a well serves as a social gathering place. Achegour had taken on the liveliness of a marketplace, thanks to the presence of the twelve men from the truck convoy. Near the well there were concrete water basins for washing clothes, and a little farther away some stones marked off a mosque area for worship. The presence in the desert of a spring that never runs dry gives people a sense of security. A well is considered a safe shelter — but even there, people are no better off than defenseless lambs, irresistibly drawn to water.

About sunset, the truck caravan split into two groups and set out again for distant horizons, one group bound for Dirkou and the other for Seguedine, still farther north. We two were left alone beside the well.

Silence had returned to the area, and we started looking around. Close behind the well was a low plateau of sand and gravel, and in front of it the immense Ténéré plain spread out endlessly. The sun was gradually setting and had lost all its strength; it was painting the whole scene crimson, and in the silence a wonderful feeling of serenity had returned. In this still world the only movement was that of the tall thin wild grasses that grew here and there, their pale blue shadows lengthening on the sand as they followed the movement of the sun. In the well the surface of the water — almost at ground level — shone dully, reflecting the darkening evening sky.

Suddenly the faint intermittent sound of an engine came drifting to us on the wind. This wasn't the time of day when one might have expected other trucks to arrive at Achegour, but even so . . . we climbed onto the roof of our car and looked across the plain. Far off in the distance we saw that two of the trucks that had left the well were standing still. Apparently they had become stuck in the sand and were trying to extricate themselves. After a while, the intermittent sounds of the trucks' engines became a single faint line of sound, which then began receding into the distance, as though being sucked up by the sand. The sun had now set, the desert was growing darker and darker, and the silence of Achegour became all the deeper.

We had never before spent a desert night in such an active place as a well. We could not have relaxed or slept peacefully with the feeling that nomads might come to draw water at any moment. But here at this single well, isolated in the middle of an empty horizon, it was almost impossible for anyone to take us by surprise. The barrier of the Ténéré protected our privacy completely, and beside us was a spring that would never run dry. How safe we felt! If the two truck caravans had reached their destination, then we two were utterly alone within a radius of 95 miles (150 kilometers).

Inside this protective barrier, I took off all my clothes and took a bath in the water. The dead and bloated body of a rat was floating on the surface, but what was that compared with the luxury of having all to oneself a spring that would keep running for all eternity? A great horned owl had swooped down from somewhere and, perching on a nearby rock, sat watching us intently.

Next morning we were up and on our way before dawn: if we wanted to get over the low hills that extended for about 2 miles (3 kilometers) beyond the well, we had to leave early while the sand was slightly damp and therefore harder.

On our third day in the Ténéré, after passing Achegour, the quality of the sand changed drastically. The flat earth vanished, giving way to a ceaseless undulation of sand dunes that spread out before us. Jumbled together as though they were vying with each other to get hold of ground that could give them even a little support, innumerable ruts wandered crazily through sand that was much softer than it had been before. Anxiety welled up within me. The reliable pair of straight ruts that had been guiding us until then suddenly became a confusing tangle. The broad road that had seemed to stretch out indefinitely had grown narrow, and our Land Rover struggled along the sandy track that had been beaten down by old-style trucks. When we finally reached the top of a gentle slope that we had felt would go on forever, there was a long sand dune, its sloping surface criss-crossed with ruts. As the sun rose higher, the scorching sand got softer and softer; it seemed white and bloated.

We started up the steep incline of the dune, and our engine went into weak convulsions, our tires digging into the sand. Afraid we might get stuck, I made a U-turn and went back down the dune the way we had come, hoping to find a harder surface for the ascent. I tried a second time, and a third, and finally we realized that there simply were no hard surfaces. We knew then that the only way we could go on was to plunge full speed into the sand. And in we went, headed for what turned out to be a long series of sand dunes.

Sometimes we could push our way to the top of a dune without stopping, but more often than not we would get stuck about halfway up. Then we would have to use the "sand plates," two strips of iron that we would put under the tires so they could get some traction. We could place the plates on the sand and drive the short distance they permitted, thus climbing in short spurts. Sometimes we would gather enough momentum to drive all the way to the top of a dune and down the other side in a single spurt. Then we would have to walk back, sometimes as much as 1,000 feet (300 meters), to retrieve the shovel and the sand plates that we had used to extricate ourselves. Walking in burning sand up to our ankles, we would pull the hot, heavy iron plates toward the car. Where our hands touched the plates, the skin peeled and cracked. We felt as though we were swimming in our own sweat.

That day the car got stuck in the sand twenty times. We felt as though we were simply wasting precious gasoline trying to climb the side of an anthill. The 100-mile (160-kilometer) trip from Achegour to Dirkou took us seven long hours.

A Camel Caravan

Early one morning in midsummer we awoke to find ourselves totally encircled by the horizon. Hastily finishing breakfast, we started off northeast, with our Land Rover dragging its shadow behind us; it was almost as though we were being pulled along relentlessly by the stark red sun as it rose about the horizon.

The day before, we had started following the tracks left by a large caravan of more than 250 camels that had set out a month ago from Abéché, in Chad, bound north for the Sabbah Oasis in Libya. The caravan had camped the night before at Al Qatrūn well, which was the last watering place before Sabhah. They were by now trekking day and night to their final destination, approximately 125 miles (200 kilometers) to the north.

We hurried after them, following the countless hoofprints and footprints that stretched out in a long straight line to the horizon. The going was easy, for the sand was harder than we had expected. We had been driving almost an hour when we saw, hovering slightly above the horizon between the brown sand and the blue sky, a great many dirty-looking dots. On drawing nearer we realized that the dots were camels. In the great desert, even as large a herd as this one could look like nothing more than dirty smudges on the distant horizon.

In the Sahara nowadays trade carried on by camel caravans is extremely limited, having largely given way to trucks. In one day a camel can walk 25 or 30 miles (40 or 50 kilometers) and carry a load of about 180 pounds (80 kilograms). Compare this with a truck. One truck with an eight-ton capacity (equal to the load of a hundred camels) can cover 300 miles (500 kilometers) a day (equal to a camel's ten days). And when you consider the labor involved in loading and unloading the camel each time it rests, feeding and watering it, to say nothing of the various expenses involved, you can see that camel transportation is far from profitable. Recently, however, the demand for camels as food has grown in the north, and this has made such caravans profitable again, for the camels can both transport merchandise and, at the journey's end, become merchandise themselves. They are sent from the grazing lands of southern Chad all the way to Libya, where the demand for their meat is great. When they reach Sabhah after a journey of more than a month, most of the animals are loaded onto trucks and are then sent off to slaughterhouses in cities along the northern coast. From the camel's point of view, there is little difference between reaching the destination or dying along the way; I felt, sentimentally, that dying on the sand beside the trail was at least a more natural, more honorable end for a camel.

In the caravan that we had overtaken the camels were divided into three groups, one behind the other, moving along under the care of nine camel drivers and a guide. From the guide — who rode about half a mile ahead of the caravan and was the only one of the men who was mounted — to the end of the last group of camels, the line of the caravan stretched out for almost 1¼ miles (2 kilometers). Except for the few camels that carried the baggage for the daily use of the drivers, the animals carried no loads. In the heat of midday, the camels would be allowed to rest and the men would eat and take naps that could last up to three hours. Then, except for a short break for the evening meal, the caravan would move along all through the night until noon the following day. Having no compasses or maps, the camel drivers took their directions from the stars at night and the sun by day. It was while the sun was directly overhead, giving no indication of direction, that they rested. The camels were not tied with ropes, and the drivers had to be constantly alert to keep the camels from straying from the line. These men had to walk about 600 miles (1,000 kilometers), keeping up with the fast pace set by the camels and not stopping even for water except at mealtimes. We were told that this caravan had originally consisted of 300 head, but the men had had to kill ten along the way; they had become disabled and couldn't keep up, and another twenty-six camels had been lost, leaving a total of 264.

You would not think so from their appearance, but camels are nervous, high-strung animals. We had no sooner driven up to greet the guide than his camel let out a bellow and went crazy. Apparently the car was too much for him to stand. Quickly the guide made the camel kneel and then began beating him from his long neck all the way down his body. Facing the angry, bellowing camel, the man gathered his strength and used the whip with all his might. He hit the camel some twenty times, and even then the animal kept on bellowing. Finally, when the man got back in the saddle and made the camel stand, it grew quiet. In order not to upset the camels further, we fell back and drove along well behind the caravan. Again, in the space between the horizon and the blue sky, we saw that strange sight of innumerable living things flickering in the shimmering heat, soundlessly moving in the air.

It was a little past ten in the morning when the camel at the end of the caravan began to falter. Attended by one of the drivers, it steadily fell farther and farther behind. As we watched, the driver started running ahead toward the front of the caravan. But no matter how fast he ran, he couldn't catch up, for it is no easy matter for a man to outstrip the fast pace of camels. Something seemed badly wrong, and we drove toward the man. When he saw us, he altered his direction and ran to meet us, panting heavily. He gestured that he wanted me to stop the caravan. So I drove up to the guide again. He quickly understood my gestures and made his camel kneel, then threw himself face down to wait in the small patch of shade made by his camel's body. The rest of the herd soon reached the spot where the guide was waiting and stopped, and after another ten minutes or so the slow camel arrived too. Aside from seeming a bit weak, there was little in its outward appearance to distinguish it from the other animals. By this time all the other camels had been made to kneel on the sand, and their legs had been fettered.

The men exchanged a few words and then separated. The one who was nearest to me mut-

tered something. I knew very little of their language but it seemed he was telling me that they were going to kill the weakened camel. Apparently they had stopped the entire caravan on purpose in order to do so. What a harsh reality — all you had to do was fall behind a little and your throat would be slit on the spot! But here in this vast expanse of sand, to slow up for the sake of one camel could easily jeopardize an entire caravan. If you do not immediately get rid of hindrances, you are courting your own death.

The weakened camel, unfettered, was standing alone about 65 feet (20 meters) away from the herd. No one was guarding it: a camel that has lost its strength won't run away. Four hours later, still in that same spot, the camel would die, blood gushing from its slit throat, released at last from further suffering.

The men unloaded their baggage and, lighting the firewood they had brought with them from the last wadi, started preparing a meal. They spread the packsaddles out on the sand and stretched a piece of cloth over them to make a patch of shade. Then, one after another, they crawled in and were soon fast asleep in the crowded space. A bit later they roused themselves long enough to finish the simple meal and then went to sleep again. Crawling back in our car, we too took refuge from the sun. All the camels kneeling there under the burning sky had their eyes wide open, but they were still and motionless. The weakened camel, still unfettered, made no attempt to approach the other camels and, after a time, knelt where it was. It was a strangely silent noon.

Two o'clock in the afternoon is the hottest part of the Libyan day, when the sun is directly overhead. Several of the men got up and got ready to kill the camel. We left our car, carrying our cameras. One of the men was honing his knife on a stone. (They all carried knives, worn in leather sheaths attached to the left arm; the knives were double-edged and about 6 inches [15 centimeters] long.) Leaving the camel kneeling just as it was, the men tied each front leg so it would stay bent and then tied the back legs to the body, thus making sure that the animal could not suddenly rise to its feet.

Surrounded by the men during this operation, the camel made no fuss at all, as though it knew what was going to happen. But when two men pulled its nose to stretch the neck out horizontally, the camel raised a howl. Since it couldn't move, that was its only protest. Another two men stood on either side and supported the kneeling body.

With his foot the man with the knife dug a small trench under the camel's neck to catch the blood. In a low voice the man murmured part of the Moslem ritual for slaughtering animals. Only meat prepared in this way, with the throat slit in the holy name of Allah, is considered fit to eat.

First, the knife was plunged into the right side of the neck. For an instant there was a glimpse of white flesh, and then this was dyed bright red. With all his strength, the man gave another thrust. Hot blood came spurting out from the severed artery as though a dam had broken. Then the man moved to the animal's left side and made another deep cut. The spurting stream of blood gurgled as it sank into the sand. The trench that had been dug was soon overflowing and the blood spread slowly over the surrounding ground. There seemed too much blood for a single body; a veritable sea had formed. Moving closer, I took a picture showing the pale blue sky, the brown sand, and the red sea of blood. Even as the crimson tide spread, commemorating the death of a camel, the desert was coming back to life within my viewfinder. In this wide, wide desert, death can be extremely vivid and real: here there is nothing gray or in-between. And then the simple ceremony of death ends and life returns. The camel had returned to the sand from which it had come.

The nauseating smell of blood filled the air around us. All this while the camel's body had been rocking back and forth in a motion that was transmitted to the bodies of the two men supporting it. The camel was rocking like this, as though to ease the pain of death, when suddenly the knife severed the tendons of the neck; with a final spasm, the camel flung its neck out and was still. Judging by their expressions, the men had taken the killing as a matter of course. Their faces showed only the same mild relief that a farmer might feel when he finally throws away a large root he has pulled out of the ground with great trouble. Now the last fresh blood was draining from the camel in weak spurts, in time to the fitful beating of its heart, and soon these stopped too. I watched the color drain from the animal's face. From one of the wide-open eyes, with dilated pupils, a few tears appeared and ran down the cheek. Within a few minutes the sea of blood that had filled and overflowed the trench had already dried up and was just a black stain on the sand.

Do animals understand death? Certainly the 263 camels that so intently watched this death of a member of their own herd gave no indication, made no sound. This was the eleventh of their herd to be killed along the way. Surely the camel must have known what was going to happen when it became unable to keep up with the others. Perhaps it continued to walk doggedly on, keeping pace with the others as long as it did, precisely *because* it knew — because they all, men and camels alike, knew.

When a camel falls behind, it has to be killed on the spot: this is a simple but inflexible law that men have agreed upon ever since Saharan caravans began moving across the sandy wastelands. Long ago, it is said, even human beings who couldn't keep up with a caravan were simply left behind to die, with no one so much as pausing to look back at the friend or kinsman they were abandoning. Such is the harsh, unbending code of the desert. To spend time over any one person, or animal, or thing, is to expose the lives of many persons to danger. In a land where this philosophy has necessarily come into being, one can't expect to find an attachment between man and animal, such as the American cowboy has for his horse. Here in the desert, man is the master; animals, the slaves — their lives, and their deaths too, are in the hands of men.

In all parts of the world animals are domesticated and their behavior shaped to suit man's needs. Men, in turn, are shaped by the conditions in which they live. As a friend of mine, a man of the desert, said: "The camel is an animal that Allah made for the use of people who travel across the desert. They are made to carry the travelers' goods and, when needed, to provide man with meat and water from their own bodies." (The water he meant was the water in the camel's hump, which has saved many a person from death by thirst.)

One of the men who was dismembering the camel suddenly turned to me and said something I could not understand, pointing at the blade of his knife and then at my car. It finally dawned on me that he was asking me for a sharp knife, for his had become blunt. I shook my head and gestured that I had no knife to lend him.

Somehow I couldn't bring myself to bring out our cooking knife. The men had cut the meat from the legs and were putting it in large bags woven from palm leaves. The legless body had been slit open at the belly and the entrails poured over the sand. One man standing over the body put his hand into the belly and, with a great wrench, pulled out a lump of meat the size of a man's head. It was the animal's heart. Turning to me, the man held the heart out to me. He seemed to be saying that he wanted to present it to me. I waved my hands in refusal.

"Why?"

As well as I could I explained in sign language that we already had more than we could eat in our car. Whether or not he understood, he must have seen the look of desperate refusal on my face, because he seemed puzzled for a moment and then handed the heart to one of his comrades. Evidently he was unable to understand that I could never have brought myself to eat that piece of meat. Even if I had been able to speak their language fluently, I doubt that I could have made them understand.

(Earlier, when they had been ready to finish the animal off, one of the men had laughed and offered me the knife, inviting me to give the death blow. When I shook my head, shocked, they had all laughed. I could tell by their faces that they were thinking: "What, you've never even killed a camel?")

After a while the butchering was over and they began preparations for departure. The meat was loaded onto the backs of the other camels, and the men cleansed their bloodstained hands in the sand. Then they all knelt and bowed in the direction of Mecca, offering devout prayers. Once they had started on their way again, there would be no time for praying. Thus, the caravan set off northward again as though nothing had happened — except that now there was one camel fewer than before. I turned and looked at the remains of the animal, a legless carcass, lying abandoned in the silence of the desert.

Our Life in the Sahara

Our living space in the desert was, quite literally, the Land Rover in which we both ate and slept. Having replenished our supplies of food and water, we would leave an oasis about the time the sun began to incline toward the west. The best resting places or campsites along the way were sand dunes where no one ever came, or the gravelly foothills in the middle of nowhere.

In its extreme aridity, the desert begins a daily process of transformation as soon as the rays of the sun begin to weaken. Even in midsummer, when the temperature at noon can reach 120° F (50° C), as soon as the shadows lengthen the mercury in a thermometer drops so fast that you can actually see it move. In the late afternoon we would spread our mattresses on the ground in the shade of the car and lie on them. Then we could feel our senses, all but overcome by the day's heat, gradually begin to relax and revive. When the horizon, which had been only a quivering shimmer of heat, finally became a fixed line, we were released from the discomfort of the long day just passed. How glad we were to be out in the open, instead of in one of the mud-walled houses that at that time of day would still be giving off the scorching heat in which they had been baked all day.

In the desert at night one is particularly conscious of the moon and stars. It was the moon, going around the earth so steadily and reliably — but all the while changing its position and shape — that gave us a vivid sense of the ceaseless flow of time. Whenever we looked into the evening sky to see a thin, threadlike moon, we would be reminded that one of our desert months had already flown by and a new one was beginning.

After eating a simple evening meal, we would lie down to rest again before beginning our journey through the night, and often we would fall asleep again, just as we were, without meaning to. Once I was awakened by the movements of a small desert rodent, a jerboa, that had bravely crawled up onto my body. Thus the early evening would pass, and by the time we had hurriedly cleaned our supper dishes and climbed into the car, the constellations would be revolving in their great, fixed orbits.

And that was our life, there in the middle of the desert. We had food and water and transportation, as long as we had gasoline. These were our only necessities, and with them we were free of all constraints, owing no one anything. We could do exactly as we liked.

But even in our life of freedom between sand and sky, there were times of hardship, times that called for great endurance. These were the nights when we were suddenly attacked by sandstorms. We had never imagined we would think so enviously about life within thick walls. Sandstorms strike with no warning at all. The most annoying ones were those of midsummer,

which would start blowing while we were relaxing in the late afternoon and preparing, or perhaps finishing, our evening meal. Everything that we had taken out of the car, except the heavy water tank, would be in danger of being carried away by the wind, and we would have to grab things and get them quickly back into the car. Then, inside the hot car with the windows all tightly shut, we would try to finish our food, now filled with sand. Fortunately, such sudden winds seldom lasted more than an hour or so, after which quiet would return to the desert. Only occasionally would the wind continue throughout the night. In the morning every surface inside the car would be covered with a film of yellow dust, and little mounds of sand would have built up beneath the slightest crack in a door or window. In short, there were good times and bad times; and there was nothing for us to do but to accept the extremes of desert conditions just as they came. And because we did learn to accept them, life in the Sahara became second nature.

Probably the most difficult ordeal we had to endure occurred in midsummer, just before leaving the Sahara, as a result of which we came to know the desert more fully than ever before. Not only were we running badly behind schedule but our money was running out as well. Our car, having been driven days and weeks on end over extremely bad roads, was gradually giving out and repair costs were mounting. Almost broke, we barely made it to the house of a friend I had made in the Igli Oasis, south of Béchar, on my first trip there.

By this time it was the end of July, the season when the sun passes directly overhead, its intense midday heat dividing each endless oasis day into two exact halves. At this time of the year, the farmers set off for their fields in the early morning while it is still dark and stop work by ten, hurrying home as though pursued by the increasing heat. They take long siestas during the hottest part of the day, patiently suffering the baking heat inside their houses until it is time for late-afternoon worship. This pattern is not limited to oasis dwellers, by any means: nomads also wait in their tents, and caravaneers in the shade of their trucks or camels. Animals, too — *all* the living things of the Sahara patiently wait, in whatever shade or shelter can be found or devised, for the sun to sink.

As for us, once we had mailed off a request for money to a Swiss acquaintance, there was nothing for us to do but to endure the stagnant heat as well, day after day. At Igli, communications with the outside world were limited to the twice-weekly bus bringing mail and passengers from the north, so after about ten days we had something better to do than simply to suffer the stifling temperatures and that was to hope each day that the next bus would bring an answer.

The bus rarely arrived on time. Sometimes it was as much as five hours late and occasionally, when it broke down, it never arrived at all. When it finally did arrive, word went round the village in a flash and everyone who had been anxiously awaiting news came crowding around. From time to time one would see someone — easy to pick out because he would be wearing his best clothes — there to meet a relative who had gone to work in the cities to the north. When they met, you would have thought they were lovers who had been separated for years as they hugged each other and kissed each other's cheeks over and over — except that they were men with beards. Usually, however, there is just a crowd waiting longingly for "something" as they trail after the mail bag that has been thrown down from the bus. Finally the postmaster reads out twenty or so names, proudly performing the important task of handling each letter to its addressee or to some friend. Then the excitement is over and people return to their homes with the air of having taken part in a major event. There might even be a few lucky ones with letters to read, but most of the people — including us — had nothing to look forward to until the next arrival of an unreliable bus.

We had been at Igli almost half a month when we had to leave our friend's house: his elder brother had come home on leave from the army, and there simply wasn't room for us in the crowded space. For the next week we had to spend our days in the shade of a palm tree by the side of a salty stream about 1¼ miles (2 kilometers) outside the village, living on the food our friend brought us. Every night, to escape the hordes of insects that thrive in and around the village, we would move the car to some sand dunes a mile or so farther on. During the day we had nothing to do but simply wait in the shade made by stretching two blankets between our car and palm tree, just like nomads inside their tents. The sweat streamed down our bodies and dripped onto the sand.

We were, in truth, captives of the desert. When the hot winds brought raging sandstorms, all we could do was lie sulking in our beds, sometimes reading books (more often, simply following the letters with our heat-weakened eyes) or belatedly lamenting the follies that had finally brought us to this pass. We covered our heads completely with clothes to protect them from the sand; our bodies lay soaked in sweat. Even though we had come to face desert conditions much as the nomads did, on such occasions our stoicism deserted us, and we cursed the midsummer Sahara. Even when we thought of fleeing northward to some nearby town, we knew it would be just a waste of our tiny hoard of gasoline: for homeless, moneyless persons, anywhere in the Sahara would be much the same. If for no other reasons than the meager shade we had, the food our friend brought us, and the diminishing hope of receiving that impossible letter, we decided we would do better to stay where we were. We had little or no choice.

Perhaps it now sounds like an exaggeration, but at that time we actually began to think that we would grow old and die in the desert just for lack of money. There was the constant sound of hot, dry breezes rustling through the palm leaves, the melancholy braying of a donkey carried to us on the wind, and then deep, deep silence. . . . You may know, literally, that you grow older each day, but it takes the fatigue and fever of the desert to make you feel this in your very bones, to feel your life slipping away into the sand.

In this way we gave a full week of our lives to the desert, and still the unreliable bus brought us no news from Switzerland. Finally we roused ourselves from our languor and sold most of our possessions. Thus we scraped together enough money for the gasoline we needed to travel the 750 miles (1,200 kilometers) through Morocco into Spain. The time had come to steal away from the Sahara, carrying with us whatever was left of our lives.

During our week of captivity under the palm trees, the image of the Sahara that had gradually entered our blood underwent a transformation. The deep lassitude that we had experienced during each hour of burning sunlight, the languor that robbed us of sensitivity toward the desert, were no longer dissipated by the silence of each gentle nightfall. Now the dark interval of night was nothing but another kind of death. The desert had lost all its poetry.

Our only solace was that of tracing letters in the books we had brought with us from Japan. Somehow, vague and disconnected as the words were as they drifted through my mind, they formed vivid images that I still remember. "Echoes in a green valley . . . the voices of deer in fog . . . mountains, rivers, grass, trees — nature . . . the sweet voices of mountain birds . . ." How gentle the world of Japan seemed to me then — and how impossibly far away. Then the brown sand of the Sahara would open before my eyes to reveal a vivid green, and in my imagination I would throw myself down upon the green earth and stretch my body to my heart's content and feel the luxury of cool breezes that came rustling through the treetops.

There was one book in particular that for some reason kept echoing through my mind — the Old Testament. It tells the parched, blood-smeared story of the struggle between God and man, set in a desert probably very similar to the one where I now languished, a history filled with the smells of blood and burning sacrifices, with greed and vengeance, sin and defilement, and above all, with the covenant between man and his jealous God. . . . I believe it was only at this point that I ceased to be a traveler and became a dweller in the desert, with an instinctive understanding of its ways.

Within another two or three days we had made our escape from the Sahara, returning to the moisture for which we had longed so ardently. The sight of the Mediterranean should have filled us with inexpressible pleasure. But instead, our bodies, so long accustomed to the aridity of the desert, shrank from the sea breezes, finding them salty and uncomfortably humid. We all but gasped for breath. The sound of the sea was nothing but a meaningless noise to our ears. And the thought of innumerable living things concealed in the forests of darkly clustered eucalyptus trees and the fields of lush grasses filled us with an almost eerie feeling of uneasiness.

Was our longing for coolness nothing but a figment of our addled brains? I may never know. Now my mind seemed to sweep away the reality of the desert, and irresistibly I was filled again with a longing for the Sahara's silence, for sand stretching endlessly toward the horizon, under a blue sky with no hot winds, no dryness. In short, within my mind an ideal Sahara already was replacing the harsh reality of a few days before. . . . Perhaps I shall be a captive of *this* Sahara all the days of my life.

CAPTIONS

1. TIMIMOUN, ALGERIA. *The last rays of the setting sun. The sun has just sunk below a horizon that is quivering in a shimmer of heat. Now, for a few minutes more, it continues to cover the earth with rays that are suddenly fresh and bright. Thus the scorching day passes through the purifying process of darkness, and the Saharan night, wrapped in gentle coolness, begins. From the mosque's minaret the words of the Koran sound resonantly through the desert air, calling the faithful to worship, and the oasis returns to life in the cool of the evening.*

2. GRAND ERG OCCIDENTAL, ALGERIA. *Sand dunes extending as far as the eye can see. The sand of the Sahara is a deep brown color, but sometimes it seems to change from one color to another with the movement of the sun. The silhouette of silver sand dunes against the glittering light of the rising sun is expressive of an infinitely gentle melancholy.*

3. KERZAZ, ALGERIA. *We enjoyed camping at the foot of sand dunes. Waking early in the morning and investigating the cool valleys between dunes, we often made discoveries. For example, early one morning I climbed a small dune and came upon this flower blooming alone in the harsh land, a small breath of life in the vastness of nature. As delicate and accidental as the plant seemed, I knew it must have an extremely long and hardy root system to exist here.*

4. GRAND ERG OCCIDENTAL, ALGERIA. *The glow of the evening sun over the dunes near the Igli Oasis. Once, while still new to the Sahara, I was walking along the ridge of a steep dune and was surprised to hear a noise almost like a low moaning. The sand, unable to support my weight, had started to slide, leaving a pattern like that seen in Photo 5, and it was this movement that was producing the sound. The sliding occurred everywhere along the ridge line where I had left footprints and became a huge chorus echoing between the walls of the surrounding dunes. This natural phenomenon usually occurs in the evening, after sandstorms have passed, and sometimes, it is said, can build up into a thundering sound that shakes the very heavens and earth.*

5. AÏN SALAH, ALGERIA. *Sand dunes cannot hold all the sand particles that are swept up on them by the wind, and the grains of sand are almost constantly sliding down the slopes to make new patterns in the sand. This is the way sand dunes gradually spread outward, acting like perpetual sand clocks.*

6. KERZAZ, ALGERIA. *A slender reed timidly pokes its head above the earth, bends down, and, propelled by a breeze, draws a fine circle in the soft sand. Meanwhile the shadow of the grass quietly and gradually grows longer.*

119

7. KERZAZ, ALGERIA. *Wind has bared the roots of a date palm and whipped away the sand that covered them. But these roots stretch down to water far below, and the tree will certainly continue to live and grow. At one oasis I was told that every single date palm that grew in the region, even those isolated trees in the nearby sand dunes, belonged to a specific owner. The history of an oasis is also the history of its relation to the date palm.*

12. AÏN SALAH, ALGERIA. *An old woman carrying a bundle on her head. This custom is widely practiced, from the Iberian Peninsula through Africa into the Middle East and India, but only in the Sahara does it seem that the darker the color of the skin and the farther south one goes, the more one encounters this custom. Men who wear turbans are unable to bear goods in this way.*

8. KERZAZ, ALGERIA. *A valley oasis in a haze of sand. Once the wind starts blowing, everything instantly changes its appearance. The ridge lines of the sand dunes, until then massively settled, start to move and billow, and the date palms bend their supple trunks restlessly from left to right. At such times one gets the feeling that the desert is suddenly waking from a long sleep. Sometimes the curtain of sand, after hovering for a moment, is carried away and disappears as gently as a piece of soft music that gradually recedes until it can no longer be heard.*

13. IGLI, ALGERIA. *A woman and her daughter-in-law weave a carpet in the inner courtyard of their house. This is a rough undercarpet, to be laid beneath the brightly colored carpets of which the people are so fond. It is especially during the month's fast of Ramadan that the women of the Sahara pour so much energy into weaving, thus distracting their minds from the irritation of thirst and hunger.*

9. TIMIMOUN, ALGERIA. *Oasis: the green of date palms and mud houses suddenly appear in the middle of a brown wasteland. In front of the nearer village are many grave markers, telling of the generations that have lived here. Such places, in the midst of the vast Sahara, are unmistakably human domains. Here people live, die, and return to the sand — a truly humble life.*

14. AL QATRŪN, LIBYA. *These men have come from the green areas of the southern Sahara to work in Libya, a country rich in oil. They are loading a truck with the many purchases — beds, radios, and so on — they have made to take on the long trip home across the desert. In addition, chickens and goats might well be piled onto the very top of the heap.*

10. OUARGLA, ALGERIA. *An old man brandishes a whip as his panting donkey plods along against a setting of sand dunes and a solitary palm tree. The gently drifting clouds are a rare sight in the desert sky. For a single instant the sun softens its angry face behind a veil of clouds.*

15. KERZAZ, ALGERIA. *A herd of goats search for clumps of grass at the foot of a giant dune. One wonders how any grass at all could grow in the endless sand. The morning I took this picture I was staying at the house of an elementary-school teacher; this was the sight that greeted me as I walked outside rubbing my sleep-filled eyes. I rushed back to get my camera, not realizing how frequently I would see this sight during my travels.*

11. IGLI, ALGERIA. *A four-month-old baby boy of the Shluh tribe, bound like a mummy and put to sleep in the shade of an inner courtyard. The binding is said to prevent babies from becoming bowlegged.*

16. KERZAZ, ALGERIA. *Most of the oases in Algeria's western Sahara have big sand dunes that seem to be drifting behind the villages. People settle wherever there is a supply of underground water or a cluster of date palms growing wild, and often such places happen to be beside dunes. Here a young man hurries home at dusk along the foot of a large dune. Another dune, from the foot of which I took the photo, casts a long shadow where he walks.*

17. DJANET, ALGERIA. *The village in the Djanet oasis seems to be crawling up the bare slope behind it. It is written in the Koran that on doomsday the earth will shake violently, and the mountains will crumble to dust and be carried away by the wind. I wonder what the people who live here think when they hear these words recited.*

22. IGLI, ALGERIA. *Moslems pray five times a day — at dawn, at noon, in midafternoon, immediately after sunset, and at night before going to bed. Hands, feet, and face are cleansed with sand if water is unavailable. While menstruating, women are considered unclean and are not allowed to read the Koran or to worship. This photo shows worship after sunset.*

18. AÏN SALAH, ALGERIA. *For men of the desert, the donkey is a more practical means of transportation than a bicycle. Sometimes one sees a small donkey carrying a huge man weighing more than 200 pounds (90 kilos). The donkey keeps on trotting through the deep sand, shaking its head back and forth but otherwise not complaining. Sometimes I wonder if these beasts do not regret having been born donkeys; their braying is reminiscent of a man sobbing.*

23. IGLI, ALGERIA. *The most beautiful sight in the Sahara was not the sand dunes or the mirages or the stars in the desert sky, but the people at their prayers. They would bow so low in worship that their foreheads, noses, and chins would actually touch the golden sand. This man has clearly forgotten us and is thinking only of his God; his very posture is of one who has communed with his Maker.*

19. IGLI, ALGERIA. *It is almost impossible for travelers to meet the young women of an oasis, for most of them are always heavily veiled when they go out. However, once a stranger is accepted into their houses as a guest, the women no longer seem restrained by the taboo. Still, it was to my wife, not to me, that these women came over to talk.*

24. IGLI, ALGERIA. *The people's graves are left without inscriptions, for Islam teaches that death is only a temporary ending of this life: at the last judgment the faithful will be restored to an eternal afterlife of perfect bliss. The grave shown here has been marked with an ordinary water jar and the charms, in leather pouches, that the dead person wore when alive.*

20. TAMANRASSET, ALGERIA. *The marketplace barber. I learned from my own experience that it is difficult to wear a turban over long hair: the head-dress keeps coming loose and slipping off. Maybe this is the reason most men in the Sahara keep their hair quite short. The Tuareg have a single tuft of long hair that sticks out of the top of the turban, but otherwise their hair too is close-cropped. The men in the photo are black Haratin.*

25. IGLI, ALGERIA. *One morning at an oasis, a villager died. His body was immediately washed and, still naked, was wrapped in a white cotton shroud and buried in the cemetery. It is forbidden to shed tears between the time of death and burial: it is said that the tears would wash the deceased into Hell. Nor are women allowed to join the funeral procession but must observe from a distance, as the two women in the lower right of this photo are doing.*

21. IGLI, ALGERIA. *After finishing their work, the men of this oasis generally rest for a while in the shade of a tree. This is especially true on hot summer days, but even in the winter they rest. When the sun has set and they have performed the ritual of evening prayers, they will set off for home.*

26. IGLI, ALGERIA. *Prayers are always said facing Mecca, which in the Sahara means eastward. Hence the Saharan worshiper never faces the sun: his first prayer after sunrise is at noon, by which time the sun is either directly overhead or slightly declining toward the west. While praying, a person sees only Allah, the one God, and is completely oblivious to things of this world, even those that occur before his very eyes.*

27. BENI ABBÈS, ALGERIA.
When its vein of underground water goes dry, an oasis dies and is abandoned. Hot winds rage over the vestiges and gradually all traces of life are covered over. Here, in a barren land that has returned to silence, only these remnants of wells stand like solemn grave markers. They were the superstructures that served as fulcrums for simple lever-type wells: long poles were set into the two slots and used as levers to draw buckets of water to the surface. The mounds of earth in front of the superstructures are the result of digging or cleaning the wells.

28. AHAGGAR, ALGERIA. *The most important lesson to be learned from desert living is adjusting one's movements to the rhythm of the sun. From the smallest insects that live on the sand to man himself, all living things are active in the cool of the mornings and evenings, but when the sun approaches its zenith, they rest and sleep. The same can be said of photography in the desert: it is most difficult to take pictures during the hottest part of the day when the desert is all but sterile, with the sun's rays raining down from above. This photo shows sunrise in the Ahaggar mountain range, a time of rest for the wild, desolate land.*

29. SOUTHERN ALGERIA NEAR IN-GUEZZAM ON THE NIGER BORDER. *Sand carried by the strong winds has eroded the bases of the boulders. The rock on the left has a big hole where the wind and sand have eaten all the way through it.*

30. HIGH IN THE AHAGGAR MOUNTAINS, ALGERIA. *Somehow Tuareg nomads manage to exist even in this wild terrain where the balance of nature is barely maintained. The men are often away, driving camels to distant Niger, leaving the women and children behind. Inside the tent are only two or three fire-blackened cooking pots, two bags of grain, and several filthy blankets. In the shade of a rock there are a couple of water bags made from old inner tubes. Needless to say, there is no water in this region.*

31. AHAGGAR, ALGERIA. *Sunrise over the top of the Ahaggar Mountains. This huge mass of basalt seems to be floating in the morning sunlight; it is almost 10,000 feet (3,000 meters) high, and Tuareg nomads live at its base, raising goats, although it often seems that it is the goats that are raising the humans. These mountains were created by volcanic activity more than two million years ago and still look more like a scene from Hell then a dwelling place for human beings.*

32. AÏR, NIGER. *Walking along a sandy riverbed in the interior of the Aïr Mountains, we came to a small village called Timia, the home of dark-skinned Tuareg engaged in farming. This old man was the local marabout, a Moslem holy man. I was impressed by his eyes as he stared fixedly at the camera. His face seems to shine with intensity of his faith.*

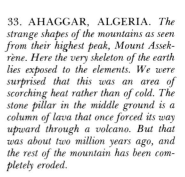

33. AHAGGAR, ALGERIA. *The strange shapes of the mountains as seen from their highest peak, Mount Assekrène. Here the very skeleton of the earth lies exposed to the elements. We were surprised that this was an area of scorching heat rather than of cold. The stone pillar in the middle ground is a column of lava that once forced its way upward through a volcano. But that was about two million years ago, and the rest of the mountain has been completely eroded.*

34–35. TAMANRASSET, ALGERIA. *Young Tuareg men. The custom of wearing a veil is not limited to the Tuareg. Other nomad tribes, such as the Maure and the Regeibat, also wear veils, but while these peoples wear them mainly to protect themselves from the sun, the Tuareg wear them because of a dislike of exposing their faces to strangers. In general, nomads are more hostile to outsiders than are people living in the oases. The Tuareg women, on the other hand, are more open than most other women of the Sahara and do not wear veils.*

36. TAMANRASSET, ALGERIA. *Tuareg nomads leading their camels to water with the sand blowing in gusts around them. Today, with the growth of automobile traffic in the Sahara, camel caravans have become extremely rare. In the old days two of the main caravan routes for the salt trade were from Bilma to Agadez in Niger and, in Mali, from Taoudenni to Timbuktu.*

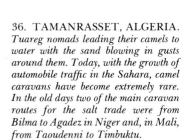

37. AGADEZ, NIGER. *Scene from a festival commemorating the founding of the republic. The main event of the day was the camel race. Usually the Tuareg ride with their feet hooked under a rope tied around the camel's neck, but once the camel starts to run this foothold becomes most precarious, and many men had to drop out of this race because they fell off their camels. The camel's body is made for walking, and the animals have to be whipped hard to be made to run, at which time their expression is truly pitiable.*

38. NEAR DOGONDOUCTCHI, NIGER. *One night on the horribly withered savanna, we were suddenly hit by a torrential rain, accompanied by thunder and lightning — an impressive announcement of the beginning of the rainy season that would turn the savanna green again. There seems to be an awesome power in the silhouettes of these huge baobab trees — their branches stretch out toward the heavens while angry flashes of lightning pierce momentarily through the jet-black darkness. Solid and triumphant, they are the majestic, dignified masters of the savanna.*

39. ANOTHER WELL NEAR TAHOUA, NIGER. *These women belong to the Bororo nomad branch of the tribal group called Fulani or, in their own language, Fulbe. Although living in negroid Africa just south of the Sahara, these people are clearly not blacks. One theory — among many — has it that their ancestors came from East Africa and ushered in the cattle-raising period depicted in the wall paintings of the Tassili-n-Ajjer.*

40. AT A WELL NEAR TAHOUA, NIGER. *Taking great care not to spill a drop, two Tuareg nomad girls pour water into a waterbag made of goatskin. Water oozes slowly through these skins, creating a process of evaporation that keeps the water inside the bags cool.*

41. WATERING PLACE NEAR TAHOUA, NIGER. *Zebu, the typical cattle of the region, crowd around a water trough. Everywhere in the green regions of the southern Sahara there are pumping stations, and these enormous domestic animals are usually found gathered around them. At the mention of cattle one usually thinks of slow-moving creatures lying around munching grass, but the cattle of this area have to be alert to survive their harsh environment. They are often hungry and thirsty, and their faces have drawn, sad expressions. Their horns may measure as much as six and one-half feet end to end.*

42. NEAR IGLI, ALGERIA. *A small well used by families of the Shaamba tribe. These people have been long in this place and even cultivate vegetables near the well. They also raise domestic animals and live in tents. Although considered nomads, they are actually settled tent-dwellers. Two days before this photo was taken there was a heavy rain; hence the dappled pattern on the sand and the footprints before the well.*

43. WATERING PLACE NEAR TAHOUA, NIGER. *The Fulbe nomads, with their cattle, were the earliest settlers anywhere in the Sahara. It is said that their intensive cattle breeding is one of the major reasons why the Sahara dried up; that the constant grazing of their cattle for many thousands of years brought the grass to an end so that today none grows anywhere in the Sahara north of the fifteenth parallel. In the central and northern parts of the Sahara, goats and camels are the principal domesticated animals, but in this area the huge zebus are the focus of nomad life. In this photo the cattle have finished drinking and are hurrying away toward the sparse shrubbery seen in the distance.*

44. TAMANRASSET, ALGERIA. *Tuareg nomads at a caravan encampment. Such men seem to spend the whole day just sitting on the sand. If they feel hungry, they gnaw on dates they have brought with them, or they just sleep, covered by a piece of cloth as protection from the sun. Only when it is time for prayers do they suddenly bestir themselves and, taking on a serious expression, pray earnestly.*

45. TAMANRASSET, ALGERIA. *A sandstorm at a caravan encampment. Having no tents, these nomads have to find what protection they can from the violently cold wind by cowering behind their luggage for several days until the storm dies down. Tamanrasset lies 4,600 feet above sea level and the temperature always descends to around 32°F. on winter nights. This storm was a long ordeal for the people; having nothing else of value, some of them sold their camels to the meat stores in town.*

46. SEGUEDINE, NIGER. *People of the Toubou or Teda tribe live in simple grass huts made of the dried leaves of the date palm. The men of the village have taken their camels to the Tibesti, in Chad, and only women and children remain at home, living quietly. The women wear a characteristic ring in the right nostril.*

47. AÏR, NIGER. *A Tuareg mother and child whom we met at the small mountain village of El-Mecki. The cross-shaped design of the mother's earrings is peculiar to the Tuareg and is also found on the men's sword hilts and the camel saddles. It is said to have originated in Byzantium.*

48. AGADEZ, NIGER. *Tuareg women singing and clapping their hands during a festival. Their lamenting voices touch the heart of a listener, but the movements of the men, still wearing their swords as they dance frantically in a circle, kicking up the sand, seem strangely out of harmony with the mood of the song. Tuareg living in the southern Sahara have intermixed with the negroid peoples of the area: note how few traces of Tuareg features appear in the face of the girl in the center.*

49. TAMANRASSET, ALGERIA. *A game resembling field hockey that is traditionally played during the festivities celebrating Mohammed's birthday. As many as three hundred men chase after the cotton ball. On this occasion, the ball rolled in among some camels at the caravan encampment, and some of the camels were hit with the playing sticks. There are no real rules to the game, but the men kept running about for almost three hours, raising sandy dust and creating a commotion throughout the town.*

50. BELOW MOUNT TAZER-ZAIT, NORTHWESTERN NIGER. *From my diary: "We are about 250 kilometers northwest of Agadez. This afternoon a sandstorm was gradually becoming worse and we couldn't even see the cars in front of us. Occasionally our field of vision would clear a bit and we could see whirlwinds moving slowly along through reddish brown clouds of sand. If the northern Sahara is the quietness after a great conflagration has reduced everything to ashes, then this region is the center of a raging prairie fire sweeping southward and roaring as it goes." Through the storm a truck can be seen pumping up water from a deep well.*

51. AHAGGAR, ALGERIA. *Stark sunlight pours down as if to pierce these pillars of basalt that the elements have thrown about in disarray, creating a veritable river of stone. Here in the mountainous Ahaggar of the mid-Sahara many different formations of stones seem to have been lined up for an exhibit. Those seen here were formed when lava cooled very quickly.*

52. NEAR IN-GUEZZAM ON THE ALGERIA–NIGER BORDER. *Traveling south from Tamanrasset one suddenly comes upon this strange site, an apparition appearing on the white, sandy horizon. At the foot of this huge mass of rock, which is about thirty meters high, is a series of prehistoric carvings.*

53, FEZZAN, LIBYA. *A camel caravan on the horizon. I used a 300 mm telephoto lens for this shot, stepping it up to 1200 mm by the use of two attachments. To get a balance between the size of the sun and the size of the camels, I went back to a point a little more than a mile away. I will never forget the scene I then beheld through my viewfinder — camels and sun in a single two-dimensional plane, the whole scene quivering in a shimmer of heat waves, the horizon undulating. Unfortunately, a still photo can only hint at all this movement.*

54. FEZZAN, LIBYA. *At about ten o'clock in the morning, when the shadows are still long and several hours remain before the noon rest period, an entire caravan has stopped for the sole purpose of killing a weakened camel that has been falling behind. Here the guide, who usually rides ahead, lies in the shadow of his camel while conferring with one of the camel drivers. The ring on top of the camel's nose is used for sighting when determining directions.*

55. FEZZAN, LIBYA. *One of the camel drivers prays after the weakened camel has been killed and butchered. The shadows are beginning to lengthen, providing directional signals without which the caravans could not find their way through the desert. In a few minutes the caravan will be under way again, one camel less.*

56. FEZZAN, LIBYA. *The caravan continues northward across the scorching sand. It is the next morning; the horizon quivers as the temperature rises, and phantasms spring up everywhere. The people and the camels are reflected in a mirage that stretches alongside the caravan like a small river, and the caravan keeps plodding along. Behind it, a single straight line, traced by the innumerable footsteps of both men and beasts, stretches back to the distant horizon.*

57. SEFAR, TASSILI-N-AJJER, ALGERIA. *A strangely shaped sandstone formation thrusts upward toward the blue sky. The rock was hollowed out at the base by torrents of rain so long ago that it defies the imagination, and it lies spread out on the desert like the intestines of some huge animal. Just standing there looking at it gave me the feeling that some heavy weight was crushing me into the sand. At the base there is the soft curved line of a gentle hill of brown sand. The Tuareg say this strange mass of stone was the work of some evil genie.*

58. TIN ABOUTEKA, TASSILI-N-AJJER. *The wall paintings of the Tassili region are drawn in the shadows on the undersides of rocks that have been eroded deeply at the base. The farther into the caves the pictures were executed, the better preserved they are; most of those that were exposed to sunlight have faded away. Here, drawn on a large scale, an archer carries a bow and arrow almost as if they were part of his body. This painting belongs to the cattle-raising period.*

61. TAN ZOUMAITAK, TASS-ILI-N-AJJER. *The white dots from the arms to the waist are scar tissue, still used by the blacks of Africa as ornamentation. This wall painting is extremely well preserved and was probably executed by an artist of the hunting period.*

59. OZANEARE, TASSILI-N-AJ-JER. *Three women are drawn on the right, and another person is lying inside a tent. For some reason Tassili painters always showed tents in cross-section, looking down from above. Here the full curves of the women's bodies are beautifully rendered. From the cattle-raising period.*

62. TI-N-TAZARÍFT, TASSILI-N-AJJER. *Night in the Tassili. This once-green plateau is now a silent, dead land. Only the constellations are the same after thousands of years, still revolving reliably in the heavens. The prehistoric men who lived in the shadow of these mountain walls possibly sat up on nights like this, frightened of the wild beasts that howled in the distance. The moon was just rising and I tried to take a long-exposure shot of our campsite. The silhouette against the rock wall at the right is a goatskin waterbag.*

60. TI-N-TAZARIFT, TASSILI-N-AJJER. *Commonly called "the swimmer," this huge painting of a person with a round head is almost 6 feet (1.8 meters) long. This is the only clearly drawn picture I found of people with round heads. The ornament on the right arm is evidently made of feathers, and there seems to be a bracelet on the left wrist. The antelope that has been drawn over the left arm is from a later period, the main painting being from the hunting period.*

63. SOUTH OF IN-AMÉNAS, ALGERIA. *Flames from a burning well in an oilfield. For a few seconds the flames billowed high in the air with a dreadful, deafening roar. But just as I was thinking they would scorch the sky, the flames, fanned by the wind, fell to earth and spread out as though to burn the sand. We stood watching this apparition for a long time, avoiding the gusts of hot air by retreating to windward each time the flames exploded high into the air. This point, about 60 miles (100 kilometers) south of In-Aménas, was our first view of modern civilization in many months.*

ACKNOWLEDGMENTS

That I was able to continue in my project of photographing the Sahara over a long period of time is owing to the support of a great many people. Among these I want particularly to express my gratitude to Mrs. and Mrs. Yoshigoro Kawasaki, Mr. Takashi Kijima, and Mr. Ichiro Fukuma, from all of whom I received not only much help but also encouragement.

Mr. and Mrs. Yoshimori Takei, of Nikon AG in Switzerland, gave me much assistance in innumerable ways during the period when I was doing research. Thanks to them I was always able to resume my travels in a refreshed frame of mind.

Mr. Zeghamri Ramdane and our many other friends in the Igli Oasis made it possible for us to come to know the everyday life of an oasis in more than a superficial way.

Mr. S. Ahmed Kerzabi, Director of the Office du Parc National du Tassili of the Algerian Office of National Parks, was particularly helpful in my researches concerning the Tassili-n-Ajjer. And I should also add a word of thanks to our Tuareg guide, Mr. Othman, who guided us in the Tassili for sixteen days.

I also received help from the staffs of the Algerian Embassy in Tokyo and the Japanese Embassy in Algeria. And I thank Peter Gantzer and Wolfram Ehlers, close friends since our chance meeting in the Sahara, for much help in Munich. Also a word of thanks to the people of the Fuji Film Professional Photo Department who helped so much in the transportation and developing of my film, and to the technicians of Nikon AG in Zurich for repairing my cameras so efficiently.

Thanks also to my good friend Yoshihiro Izukura, who was my companion on my first Sahara trip, and to Kenji Ishida, who helped me with affairs in Tokyo while I was in the field, and to my wife Shigeko, who has crossed the Sahara back and forth with me since 1973. Finally, deep thanks to Mr. Tohru Tanabe of Heibonsha in Japan and Mr. Enzo Angelucci of Mondadori in Italy for making possible the international publication of this book.

K.N.